Brian Stuart

GÄSTRIKLAND
HÄLSING-
LAND
UPPLAND
DALARNA
VÄSTMANLAND
SÖDERMANLAND
VÄRMLAND
NÄRKE
ÖSTER-
GÖTLAND
GOTLAND
ÖLAND
SMÅLAND
BLEKINGE
SKÅNE
HALLAND
VÄSTER-
GÖTLAND
DALS-
BO-
LAND
HUS-
LAN

GOOD FOOD IN
SWEDEN

The Swedish "Smörgåsbord" is a national institution which has become known all over the world, and has tempted many to try their hand at Swedish style cooking.

The collection of recipes in this book features specialties from all the Provinces of Sweden and can be viewed as a love letter to the ancient cooking traditions of this country.

As a professional cook, who owned a famous restaurant in Stockholm, Oskar Jakobsson gathered material during numerous trips all over Sweden and personally tested all the recipes, both old and new, as examples of true Swedish country cooking.

GOOD FOOD IN
SWEDEN

A Selection of Regional Dishes

Collected by
OSKAR JAKOBSSON

Illustrated by
YLVA KÄLLSTRÖM-EKLUND

BERGH PUBLISHING, Inc.
New York

ISBN 91-7077-008-5 (Sweden)
ISBN 0-930267-15-X (USA)

Grateful acknowledgment is made for permission to reprint
previously published material:
By way of an introduction etc. (pg. I—XXVII) from:
A small treasury of Swedish food from SMR, The Swedish Dairies
Association and The Swedish Farmers Meat Marketing Associaton.
Pen Drawings by Axel Bengtsson.

Printed in Sweden: Vänersborgs Offset AB, 1990

By way of an introduction

Most people associate Swedish food with the Swedish *smörgåsbord* which is world-famous for its variety of tasty dishes. But the Swedish table has a great deal more to offer. We have a number of genuine national dishes, well worth discovering. Some may seem a bit strange to you, but if you have the opportunity of tasting them, you will be agreeably surprised.

Visitors to our country are usually invited to try salmon in various forms, bleak roe (red caviar) and such "exotic" delicacies as reindeer meat and cloudberries. But there is also typical home fare, everyday dishes which have been favourites for generations, and which you may be able to make for yourself at home. These include meatballs, tiny thin pancakes, fried *strömming* (small Baltic herring), fried salted herring, pea soup with pork, and *kalops* (a nourishing beef stew).

Sweden also has a large number of provincial specialties which are cherished in certain regions, many of them are now available in food stores all over the country. The curd cake, *ostkaka*, has made its way from farm kitchens to the supermarkets. From the south of Sweden comes the *spettekaka,* a pyramid cake baked on a spit. It is made from eggs and sugar and melts in the mouth. Smoked flatfish, *gotlandsflundror,* is a specialty from the island of Gotland, which can now be found on the mainland. And many provincial types of sausages are now sold nationally.

Dairy products have by tradition played an important part in the Swedish diet. Milk has always been the customary drink taken with meals, particularly everyday meals. Some people drink

I

milk because they know it is beneficial, but most do so simply because they like it. You will see big strong Swedes with a glass of milk. Maybe that is why they are so big and strong!

Bread is nearly always spread with butter, and normally the butter is salted. Extra salt butter is sold in a red package and regular butter in a golden package. The unsalted butter, which represents a very small part of the consumption, is sold in a green package. The Rune Brand which you will find on all butter packages, is a quality mark which tells the consumer that the butter has passed the governmental butter control.

Sweden is also a cheese country par excellence. There are more than 200 different varieties of cheese, and consumption has been growing rapidly and continuously during recent years.

The following pages will take you on a short gastronomic tour, giving you a glimpse of Swedish customs as well as a chance to sample some of our favourite dishes. You will find both the homely everyday fare and the more festive food traditionally served on special occasions through the year. There are also recipes, should you want to try one or more of these dishes in your own kitchen.

Good food around the clock

Mealtimes and eating habits vary from one country to another. In Sweden they also tend to vary from one family to another. In olden times the principal meal was at noon, with a light supper early in the evening. As years went by dinner at five or six became more customary, when the whole family gathered around a rather heavy and elaborate meal. Nowadays of course meals are planned to suit modern living. With both husband and wife working outside the home, as is very often the case in Sweden, fixed hours may be difficult to keep. Meals have to be easy, quickly prepared, and yet nutritious and tasty.

Breakfast is too often a rather hasty meal before rushing off to work or to school and most people have adopted the continental breakfast of coffee or tea with bread, butter and cheese. But breakfast can also mean cornflakes or other cereals, with milk. Either just plain milk, or the fermented milk of which Swedes are so fond. Or yoghurt which has also become popular.

Lunch is served around noon and for many people it is the main meal of the day. All children have a free hot meal at school while many employees get a subsidized lunch in canteens or in quick-service restaurants, as the time is often too short to allow them to return home. The Swedish lunch is a light meal with just one hot dish and usually a glass of milk. A cup of coffee completes the meal.

Dinner is supposed to be served around five or six. But this is of course wishful thinking when the husband and wife do not stop work in town until five or six and the family lives in the suburbs. The family dinner is not what it used to be. Just a main dish of meat or fish with potatoes, and perhaps fruit and a piece of cheese for dessert. More elaborate and fancy cooking is saved for the week-end and holidays. And, indeed, many husbands prove to be excellent amateur chefs.

Anytime is coffee time

Traditionally the English drink tea whereas the Swedes drink coffee. Coffee is a part of social life. There isn't a problem which is not better solved over a cup of coffee, nor a visitor who is not greeted with the words, "Would you like a cup of coffee?" The coffee break is an institution at work and a cup of coffee ends each meal. We don't take milk with our coffee, we drink it black or with cream.

The Swedish "smörgås" or sandwich

Swedes don't eat a piece of plain bread with their food as is often the custom abroad. Instead there is a *smörgås* for almost any occasion, with or without other food. A *smörgås* is an open sandwich, but not usually the elaborate kind. It may be just a slice of bread with butter and a slice of cheese, or sausage, or ham, or whatever you find in the refrigerator. You eat *smörgås* with your morning coffee, as a hasty lunch if time is short, as an in-between snack, with some hot soup, with a glass of milk, in the middle of the night if you cannot sleep. And a pile of them is fine for picnics. The traditional Swedish loaf is often made with treacle (molasses) but nowadays, largely due to the influence of the immigrants, there is a great variety of unsweetened bread in the shops. In addition there is the Swedish *knäckebröd,* the dry crisp bread.

Tasty souvenirs to take home

Recipes for a number of Swedish dishes have been collected in this book. If you want to try them at home, you may find that many of the ingredients are available in well-stocked stores in your own country. But it may be fun to take some of them back home with you – as souvenirs!

• *Ansjovis* – Swedish anchovies are small pickled herrings with a sweet-and-sour spicy taste. Available whole or in fillets, store the cans in a refrigerator. *Ansjovis* are the main ingredient in the popular supper dish called *Janssons frestelse* (Mr. Jansson's temptation!). *Ansjovis* also belong on the *smörgåsbord*. Egg slices and *ansjovis* on bread make a very popular *smörgås*.

• *Knäckebröd* (crisp bread) is a dry bread which keeps well. It used to be called "hard bread", baked once a year and kept all through the winter. The modern varieties are very numerous, and all are very crisp.

• *Ostkaka* (curd cake) is a very special dessert made from fresh curds and eggs and baked in the oven. Serve it with jam or berries, and why not add a dollop of whipped cream. Delicious!

• *Pepparkakor* are highly spiced thin gingerbread biscuits (cookies). These are baked in nearly every Swedish home for Christmas. But you can get them all the year round. Try them with coffee – and with fermented milk or cream.

• *Ärtsoppa* – the traditional Thursday pea soup. It can be obtained in cans, ready to heat with water added. Also try adding some thyme and marjoram, and you could invite a Swedish friend!

• Cheese – Sweden is a country rich in cheeses and there are many kinds from which to choose. The typical Swedish cheese is a hard cheese. The range runs from the stronger ripened cheeses, such as *Västerbotten* and *Lagrad Svecia,* to milder cheeses such as *Grevé* and *Herrgårdsost,* and a spiced cheese like *Krydd-*

ost. There is also a selection of dessert cheeses.

• Herbs – dried marjoram and thyme – for the pea soup. Add just a pinch of each to Swedish meat balls. A glass jar of dried *dill* is easy to carry and they say dillweed doesn't grow anywhere else with such a strong flavour as in Scandinavia.

• Salted herrings for pickling or frying are available in cans, to be stored in the refrigerator.

• Smoked reindeer meat is a delicacy from the north of Sweden. It is usually sold sliced in vacuum-sealed plastic wrapping. It should be stored in a refrigerator, but with the speed of modern travel you will have no problem in taking some home with you.

The Swedish smörgåsbord

The Swedish *smörgåsbord* is of course famous all over the world although some people in other countries may have rather hazy ideas as to what should be served and how. If you visit Sweden you will have a chance of trying it yourself and telling your friends about it.

The large *smörgåsbord* served in many restaurants includes a number of different dishes. This *smörgåsbord*, originally intended as an elaborate hors d'œuvres, is in reality a kind of buffet meal. You will hardly be able to eat a hearty main dish afterwards although you may possibly manage a light dessert.

The idea is not to pile on your plate a mixture of all the various dishes set out so temptingly on the centre table. You should make several trips, starting with the herring. There are any number of different varieties. Don't miss herring with a boiled potato, fermented cream and chives. Mmmm! Now for a clean plate and another trip to the table. You will make several.

A largescale *smörgåsbord* will include salmon, both boiled and smoked. The *gravad lax*, which is salmon marinated with dill, is gaining great favour internationally. Eel, *böckling* (smoked Baltic herring) and shrimps also belong in the fish section of the *smörgåsbord*.

Other dishes which form part of a *smörgåsbord* are all kinds of cold meats, sausages, smoked reindeer meat, liver pâté, eggs, salads etc. etc.

Cheese served as part of a *smörgåsbord* should preferably be of the well-ripened type, such as *Västerbotten, Svecia* and *Kryddost*. Last but not least come the small dishes, such as *Janssons frestelse*, small meatballs, scrambled eggs, oven-baked omelettes with a choice of fillings, and tiny fried sausages.

All through the meal you can choose from a variety of vegetables, sauces, pickles and other condiments.

In many restaurants you will find a *mini-smörgåsbord* called *Smör, ost och sill* (Butter, cheese and herring). This is *the* typical Swedish hors d'œuvre. As a rule it is a small plate of herring with bread, butter and a piece of well-ripened cheese.

The traditional, largescale *smörgåsbord* is rare in private homes nowadays. If you are invited to Swedish friends they might instead start the meal with one or more specialties. Pickled herring is sure to be included. Possibly prepared by the lady of the house according to a family recipe, though the stores have all kinds in cans and glass jars. Small fried meatballs, an oven-baked omelette with a fancy filling and the very popular *Janssons frestelse* are often included. Or this latter may be served later on as a quick late-night supper, just before the guests leave.

Spring

Let us start with the *semla,* a special bun associated with Lent. This big bun, made from wheat flour, is split and filled with almond paste and whipped cream. It can be served with coffee or in a bowl with hot milk and cinnamon. These buns are so popular that they begin to appear immediately after Christmas, an indication, perhaps, of the Swedes' eagerness to forget winter and look forward to spring.

Lady Day, the feast day of the Annunciation, also has its special treat: waffles with jam and cream.

Easter has traditional fare of its own. There are eggs aplenty. Hard-boiled eggs are often fancifully decorated by the children of the family while other egg dishes are served on Holy Saturday. (Incidentally, eggs and pickled herring go well together.) The main dish on Easter Sunday is often a Leg of lamb.

On April 30 (Walpurgis night) Sweden takes leave of winter and welcomes spring, with public and private festivities. Bonfires are lighted in many places all over the country. People gather to watch the fires and to welcome the spring with songs and speeches.

Friends and relatives get together to celebrate the end of a long winter with good food and, perhaps, dancing. Typically the main dish would be *gravad lax.* For this, fresh salmon is marinated in nothing but salt, sugar, pepper and plenty of fresh dillweed. It is allowed to stand in a cold place for a couple of days, and is then ready to serve with a special mustard sauce. (For the recipes see page 136.) You may find this a strange way to prepare fish, but we assure you that it becomes tender and delicately flavoured. Other fatty fishes such as mackerel may also be prepared in the same manner.

However, many people prefer smoked fish, which is served cold or heated in the oven. With any kind of smoked fish you should try a green sauce: fermented cream spiced with one or more finely chopped fresh herbs, such as chives, dill, parsley and maybe some chopped spinach.

Summer

Every Swede turns into a poet when he talks of summer. And no wonder. Summer is short but filled with delight. Sunny days and long light evenings, glorious sunsets, glittering waves and blue sky. Strolling in green woods, swimming, sailing. Colourful gardens and wild flowers in profusion.

The Swedes also wax lyrical when thinking of such summer delicacies as the first tender vegetables. Green peas, tender beetroots and carrots should just be barely cooked in boiling water, and served with butter. But tender vegetables are also necessary ingredients in the old-fashioned soup known as *ängamat* (meadow food).

Midsummer is celebrated at the end of June. By then the first delicate new potatoes have appeared. We like to boil them with some dill, and eat them with a pat of butter. Together with *matjessill* (sweet-pickled herring), fermented cream and chopped chives they belong to the traditional lunch on Midsummer's Day. Fresh strawberries are also to be found at this time of the year. The season for soft fruit is quite long, as they ripen early in the south of the country and late in the north. Swedes eat soft fruit as often as they can, beginning with the strawberries and

moving on to raspberries, blueberries and cloudberries. In the summer children go picking *smultron,* wild strawberries which have a wonderfully concentrated taste, not matched anywhere else, because they ripen so slowly. You may find *smultron* in the market places and in some restaurants. If you do, don't miss them!

Fermented milk products are consumed in considerable quantities during the summer. The hotter the summer the larger the consumption. The regular fermented milk is *filmjölk,* but low-fat fermented milk and *yoghurt* are gaining in popularity. *Långfil* (long milk),

which has a very special consistency, comes originally from the northernmost part of Sweden. It has moved south together with many of the inhabitants from the northern provinces.

You can easily make your own fermented milk — see recipe on page 137. A bowl of this is delicious with a few gingerbread biscuits, or sprinkled with ginger and sugar. If made at home, the fermented milk will have the consistency of custard. The fermented milk you buy in cartons is more liquid, and is often served for breakfast or lunch with cereals and sandwiches.

Autumn

The 8th of August is a magical date in Sweden – this is when the crayfish season starts. Many gay parties are based on these delicious shellfish from streams and lakes, and in most cases the only food served is crayfish with bread, butter and cheese (usually the spicy *Kryddost*). In recent years Swedish crayfish have become scarce and consequently very expensive. Deepfrozen ones imported from other countries and cooked in the Swedish way with large quantities of dill, have helped the Swedes to keep up their crayfish tradition.

Autumn is also the season for other shellfish. There are small delicate shrimps, and later on crabs appear on the market.

But autumn has even more to offer in the way of food. Fresh Swedish lamb becomes available. There is of course fruit in abundance and also mushrooms, of which there are many species growing wild in the woods. Last but not least there are the typical Swedish red *lingon*-berries and the yellow *hjortron* (cloudberries). The Swedish *allemansrätt* (right of common access) entitles anyone to wander over land and through forests, and to pick berries and

mushrooms for themselves. Swedes are brought up from childhood to make use of what nature provides and to lay in stocks for the winter, so a favourite pastime on beautiful autumn days is to stroll through the woods picking mushrooms and berries.

Mushrooms can be fried in butter and used in stews and sauces or served with various meat dishes. *Kantareller* (chantarelles) is a favourite you may find in restaurants.

Most of the *lingon*-berries are made into jam, of which the Swedes consume considerable quantities all through the year. *Lingon*-berry jam is served with pancakes and waffles, but also with meat dishes and puddings. It can also be served as a dessert with milk, while *lingon*-berry juice makes a refreshing drink. The *hjortron* which grow in the northern regions also make a delicious jam.

Winter

During the cold Swedish winter hot satisfying food is particularly enjoyed. The most Swedish of soups – pea soup – is included on many menus every Thursday throughout the winter. Pea soup is made from dried yellow peas, which are boiled for a long time together with lightly salted pork. Thyme and marjoram give the soup a special flavour. Although pea soup is really a meal in itself, it is traditional to follow it with thin pancakes and jam, or the small pancakes called *plättar*.

Another dessert which is much appreciated after a soup main course is curd cake. Formerly this cake or pudding was only served on very festive occasions, and large quantities of milk,

eggs and cream went into the making. Most people now buy curd cake ready to serve. It can be heated slightly, before serving with jam or soft fruit and, preferably, with a dollop of whipped cream. You can make your own curd cake using cottage cheese as a basis. The recipe is given on page 24.

Other Swedish specialties which are popular during the winter are stewed brown beans with fried pork, and lightly salted meat which is boiled and served with mashed potatoes or mashed turnips. The most common fish dish is fried *strömming* (Baltic herring) which can be had all the year around. Any fried *strömming* left over can be marinated in vinegar and served cold the next day.

Plain boiled potatoes are, by tradition, served with Swedish everyday fare. In olden days potatoes, cabbage and carrots were practically the only vegetables available in winter, and the main source of vitamin C.

Baked potatoes have, in recent years, also become popular, particularly in younger families. They are served with various meat dishes and with spiced butter or as a dish on their own. When you split them open, fill the cavity with some very cold fermented cream, and top them with anchovies, bleak roe or caviar, with some chopped onion. Or with shredded smoked reindeer meat.

Christmas in Sweden

The Swedes really make the most of Christmas, coming as it does in the middle of our cold and dark winter. Preparations tend to start earlier each year, and the Christmas season, in fact, is not quite over until the twentieth day after Christmas day, when the Christmas tree is plundered of its decorations, and thrown out into the snow.

Christmas in Sweden, as elsewhere, is a time for good food and plenty of it. Certain traditional food is prepared according to recipes which have been handed down for generations. And though modern families have neither the time nor the inclination to spend as much time in the kitchen as in the good old days, there are some dishes and pastries which must be homemade.

Christmas dinner is served on Christmas Eve, which is also the day gifts are exchanged. Almost all Christmas tables include a Christmas ham, which will be the mainstay for other meals during the holidays. The ham is usually lightly salted and boiled or baked in the oven. Some kind of boiled cabbage will often accompany the ham. Shredded red cabbage is given a sweet-and-sour taste. The common cabbage is shredded and browned. And the bright green kale is finely chopped and cooked as spinach. Regional and family traditions decide the choice. On the traditional Christmas table there will be many of the *smörgåsbord* dishes, such as a herring salad with pickled beetroot, small meatballs, sausages, brawn, liver pâté etc.

Lutfisk is served to counterbalance the heavier fare. This is dried ling, which has been soaked in lye (to make it soft and palatable) and then boiled. It is served with a béchamel sauce, mustard, boiled potatoes and green peas.

A thick rice porridge is sometimes served to end a meal of *lutfisk,* or as a supper dish on Christmas Eve. The rice is boiled in milk, with cream, and is served with sugar, cinnamon and a pat of butter. One single almond may be added. Whoever gets it will be married within the year. And you should not forget to put out a bowl of porridge for the *tomte,* the sprite with a red cap who is the guardian of the house!

If there is any cold porridge left, it is

mixed with whipped cream. Served with fruit syrup or orange sections this makes an attractive dessert.

Christmas baking is almost as important as the Christmas food. Even those who never bake on other occasions like to bake cakes and biscuits for Christmas. The increase in butter sales when Christmas baking starts is an indication of this seasonal baking boom!

Pepparkakor (spicy gingerbread biscuits) are often baked according to family recipes. You can also buy ready-made dough in the stores. Even the little children help by making gingerbread stars and hearts and men and goats, and all the other traditional designs.

Mandelmusslor are tart shells baked in small fluted baking tins. Just before serving they are filled with jam and topped with whipped cream.

Saffron-flavoured bread is a specialty reserved for Christmas. It is made from fine wheat flour and gets its attractive flavour and colour from saffron. This bread is first served on Lucia Day, December 13, in the form of *lussekatter.*

Lucia Day is celebrated in many Swedish homes, schools, offices, hospitals etc. when, early in the morning, a Queen of Light together with her retinue of pretty maids will appear. Coffee with *lussekatter* and *pepparkakor* will be served and Christmas carols sung. Nobel prize winners, arriving in Stockholm to collect their prizes at this time of the year, often take home unforgottable memories of these radiant young girls and their Christmas songs.

The hot Christmas cordial is called *glögg.* On page XIX you will find the original recipe for *glögg* and also learn how to make *mumma,* the modern version of the Vikings' mead, which is a traditional Christmas beverage.

And so the Swedish food year comes to a close with Christmas and the New Year celebrations. The recipes given in the following pages may, perhaps, include a dish or dishes which will inspire you to experiment in Swedish cooking. Good luck!

Mumma

Mix 3 chilled bottles of Porter type beer with 2 bottles of any dark beer and approx. 1 dl of Madeira. Add a bottle of *sockerdricka* for sparkle, or any slightly sweetened carbonated water (Sprite f.ex.), but don't use soda or mineral water. Serve at once in a tall glass pitcher.

Glögg

(Hot Christmas cordial)

Pour into a saucepan 1 bottle ordinary red wine and 1/2−1 dl schnapps (or vodka or similar spirits). Add the following spices: one ginger root (whole), two pieces of stick cinnamon, 1/2 tsp cardamon seed and 6−8 cloves. Let stand and draw. Meanwhile prepare 1 dl seedless raisins and 1/2 dl blanched almonds. To serve, heat the cordial almost to the boil. Pour it piping hot over raisins and almonds in small mugs or glasses.

Some plain facts about Swedish dairy and meat products

A wide range of dairy products

Milk and dairy products have always played an important part in the Swedish diet. Milk is still the most common drink with family meals. The milk is homogenized, standardized and pasteurized. *Mjölk* (regular milk) contains 3% fat, while *lättmjölk* (low fat milk) contains only 0.5% fat.

Fermented milk products are a Swedish specialty. They have a slightly acid, agreeable and refreshing taste, and they can be used both as a beverage and as a dish by itself. The fermented cream makes wonderful dressings and cold sauces.

Filmjölk (regular fermented milk) is obtained by adding a culture of natural lactic acid to regular milk. In recent years the regular fermented milk has been joined by a low-fat variety, known as *lättfil*, which has only 0.5% fat. The

A choice of cheeses

The Swedes are among the world's most avid cheese eaters and there are about two hundred different Swedish cheeses. These are some of the most popular kinds:

Herrgårdsost is the most widely sold cheese in Sweden. It is a hard cheese with round holes. Young *Herrgårdsost* cheese is soft, pliant and mild in taste, but it ripens with age.

Greve– the Swedish equivalent to Emmentaler. The consistency is soft and pliant. *Greve* has a sweet and nutty flavour.

Drabant is a mild breakfast cheese with a slightly sour taste.

Västerbotten takes a long time to mature. It has a rich and strong aromatic flavour with a pungent taste.

Svecia is the collective name for the numerous local cheeses which were formerly made in various parts of fermented cream variety is called *grädd-fil*. Mixed with herbs, spices or other condiments it makes tasty sauces and dressings, and is also used in cooking and baking.

Local fermented milk products can be found in various parts of Sweden. A specialty from the north of Sweden is *långfil* (long milk) which has a very special consistency.

Yoghurt has become extremely popular in recent years. It is available in various fruit flavours as well as plain.

In the Swedish word *smörgås,* the first part, *smör,* means butter. We nearly always butter our bread, and Swedish butter is of a very pure and high quality. It is marked with a rune sign and known as Swedish Rune Brand butter. Almost all butter sold in this country is salted – only a very small quantity is unsalted.

The Swedish dairy industry has also developed some interesting new products, which legislation classifies as margarine. *Bregott* is composed of 4/5 milk fat and 1/5 soyabean oil. The soyabean oil makes *Bregott* spreadable at refrigerator temperature and gives it a high content of poly-unsaturated fat. *Lätt & Lagom* is a low fat margarine and contains only 40% fat compared with the 80% in butter and *Bregott. Lätt & Lagom* is manufactured from milk fat, soyabean oil and a concentrate of buttermilk protein. Since it has a high water content, it cannot be used for cooking. Sweden. It is available in every conceivable form, high-fat or low-fat, spiced or unspiced, very mild or extremely ripe.

Hushållsost is a hard cheese, cylindrical in shape. There are varieties that differ in weight and fat content. It has a somewhat granular consistency and the taste is mild and slightly sour.

Kryddost is a *Svecia* spiced with caraway and cloves.

Cheddar was of course originally an English cheese, but you should try the Swedish variety, called Kvibille Cheddar, which is rich and aromatic.

Processed meat products

Charkvaror is the Swedish name for meat products which have been treated in some way, e.g. have been smoked, salted, cooked, dried. Many of these products have an old provincial character, while others have grown out of present day demands for long keeping and convenience foods. Extremely high quality control standards are applied to the raw materials and to hygiene in the manufacture of processed meat products.

Smoked sausage is available in many varieties. *Falukorv* is the largest selling cured meat product in Sweden, and is made from beef and pork (*korv* is the Swedish word for sausage). *Falukorv* is one of the mainstays of Swedish home-cooking. It is often served fried, but can also be boiled or grilled and is excellent with vegetables.

Isterband is one of the really genuine Swedish sausages, which has no counterpart in any other country. It has a fresh and slightly sour flavour and a clear taste of smoke. It is also available unsmoked. *Isterband* contains beef, pork, potatoes, barley, onion and spices. It is fried, grilled or roasted and is served with, for example, potatoes in white sauce or mashed potatoes.

Femmarker has also a clear smokey taste. This sausage contains beef and pork, boiled potatoes, lard, milk and spices. It is mostly used for open sandwiches but is also delicious fried and served with eggs, potatoes or vegetables.

Ystad korv has a somewhat coarser consistency than *Femmarker* sausage. It is smoked over a juniper fire and has a slightly sour flavour and a marked taste of smoke. Excellent on open sandwiches and in salads.

Spickekorv contains the same raw materials as the other sausages, but is pickled and dried in the air. This gives the sausage its typical white skin. Excellent on open sandwiches and together with beer.

Black pudding and blood sausage are made from blood, fat, rye flour, onions and spices. These products are fried in slices and served with *lingon*-berry jam and a raw vegetable salad of grated carrot and cabbage. Since black pudding and blood sausage are an excellent source of iron they are often used in Swedish everyday fare.

Sylta (Veal brawn) contains veal and pork, stock and spices. Veal brawn is usually sold in small dishes and ready to eat, but there is also an excellent canned variety to take home with you. It is served on a *smörgåsbord* or as a lunch dish with pickled beetroot and boiled potatoes.

Your guide to Swedish menus

Swedish	English	German	French
Ansjovis	Anchovy	Anschovis	Anchois
Apelsin	Orange	Apfelsine	Orange
Apelsinjuice	Orange juice	Apfelsinensaft	Jus d'orange
Blomkål	Cauliflower	Blumenkohl	Chou-fleur
Blåbär	Blueberries	Blaubeeren	Airelles
Broiler – kyckling	Broiler–chicken	Hühnchen	Poulet
Bröd	Bread	Brot	Pain
Bröd, hårt	Crisp bread	Knäckebrot	Crack-pain
Bröd, rostat	Toast	Geröstetes Brot – Toast	Pain grillé
Buljong	Bouillon	Kraftbrühe Bouillon	Consommé (Bouillon)
Champinjon	Mushroom	Champignon	Champignon
Choklad – kakao	Chocolate–cocoa	Schokolade – Kakao	Chocolat
Citron	Lemon	Zitrone	Citron
Dill	Dill	Dill	Aneth
Dryck	Drink	Getränk	Boisson
Efterrätt	Dessert	Dessert (Nachtisch)	Dessert
Filé	Fillet	Lendenschnitte – Filé	Filet
Filmjölk	Fermented milk	Schweden Milch – Saure Milch	Lait caillé
Frukost	Breakfast	Frühstück	Petit déjeuner
Frukt	Fruit	Obst	Fruit
Förrätt	Hors d'œuvre	Vorspeisen	Hors d'œuvre
Glass	Ice cream	Eis	Glace
Griskarré	Loin of pork	Schweinekamm	Carré de porc
Griskött	Pork	Schweinefleisch	Porc
Grädde	Cream	Sahne	Crème
Grädde, vispad	Whipped cream	Schlagsahne	Crème fouettée
Gräddfil	Cream, fermented	Sauere Sahne	Crème fraiche
Gräslök	Chives	Schnittlauch	Ciboulette
Grönsaker	Vegetables	Gemüse	Légumes
Grönsallad	Lettuce	Kopfsalat	Laitue romaine
Gröt	Porridge	Grütze	Gruau
Gurka	Cucumber	Gurke	Concombre
Hallon	Raspberries	Himbeeren	Framboises
Hjortron	Cloudberries	Berghimbeeren	Fausse-mûre
Hummer	Lobster	Hummer	Homard
Huvudrätt	Main course	Hauptgericht	Plat

Jordgubbar	Strawberries	Erdbeeren	Fraises
Kaffe	Coffee	Kaffee	Café
Kalvkött	Veal	Kalbfleisch	Veau
Keso – Kvarg	Cottage cheese	Speisequark	Fromage blanc
Korv	Sausage	Wurst	Saucisson – Saucisse
Kotlett	Cutlet	Kotelette	Côtelette
Kräftor	Crayfish	Krebse	Ecrevisses
Kött	Meat	Fleisch	Viande
Kött, rökt	Smoked meat	Räucherfleisch	Viande fumée
Köttbullar	Meat balls	Fleischklösse	Boulettes de viande
Lammkött	Mutton	Hammelfleisch	Mouton
Lax	Salmon	Lachs	Saumon
Lax, rökt	Smoked salmon	Räucherlachs	Saumon fumé
Leverpastej	Liverpaste	Leberpastete	Pâté de foie
Lingon	Lingonberries	Preiselbeeren	Airelles rouges
Lunch	Lunch	Mittagessen	Déjeuner
Lök	Onion	Zwiebel	Oignon
Marmelad	Marmalade – jam	Marmelade	Confiture
Middag	Dinner	Abendessen	Diner
Mjölk	Milk	Milch	Lait
Morötter	Carrots	Mohrrüben	Carottes
Nötkött	Beef	Rindfleisch	Bœuf
Ost	Cheese	Käse	Fromage
Ostkaka	Curd cake	Quarkkuchen	Gâteau au fromage blanc
Pannkaka	Pancake	Eierkuchen	Crêpe
Peppar	Pepper	Pfeffer	Poivre
Pepparkaka	Gingerbread cake or cookie	Pfefferkuchen	Pain d'épice
Pepparrot	Horseradish	Meerrettich	Raifort
Persilja	Parsley	Petersilie	Persil
Potatis	Potatoes	Kartoffeln	Pommes de terre
Potatismos	Mashed potatoes	Kartoffelmus – Purée	Purée de pommes de terre
Päron	Pear	Birne	Poire
Renkött	Reindeer meat	Rentierfleisch	Viande des Rennes
Revbensspjäll	Spare ribs	Schweinerippe	Côtes de porc
Räkor	Shrimps	Krabben	Crevettes
Salt	Salt	Salz	Sel
Sill, inlagd	Pickled salted herring	Marinierte Heringe	Hareng mariné
Skinka	Ham	Schinken	Jambon
Smör	Butter	Butter	Beurre
Smör, rört	Creamed butter	Schaumbutter	Beurre battu
Smör, smält	Melted butter	Zerlassene Butter	Beurre fondu

Swedish	English	German	French
Socker	Sugar	Zucker	Sucre
Soppa	Soup	Suppe	Soupe (potage)
Spenat	Spinach	Spinat	Epinards
Spettekaka	Pyramid cake	Baumkuchen	Gâteau en pyramide
Strömming	Baltic herring	Ostseehering	Petit hareng
Sås	Sauce	Sauce	Sauce
Te	Tea	Tee	Thé
Tomat	Tomato	Tomate	Tomate
Tomatjuice	Tomato juice	Tomatensaft	Jus de Tomates
Tårta	Layer cake	Torte	Gâteau
Vitkål	White cabbage	Weisskohl	Choux blanc
Vitlök	Garlic	Knoblauch	Ail
Ägg	Egg	Ei	Œuf
Ägg, löskokt	Soft boiled egg	Weiches Ei	Œuf à la coque
Ägg, stekt	Fried egg	Spiegelei	Œuf sur le plat
Äggröra	Scrambled eggs	Rührei	Œufs brouillés
Äpple	Apple	Apfel	Pomme
Ärter	Green peas	Erbsen	Petits pois
Öl	Beer, ale	Bier	Bière

Conversion table

The figures given are approximate

Swedish	British	American
1 kg (1000 g)	2.2 lb	2.2 lb
1/2 kg (500 g)	1 lb 1 1/2 oz	1 lb 1 1/2 oz
1 hg (100 g)	3 1/2 oz	3 1/2 oz
	roughly	roughly
25 g	1 oz (1 tbl)	1 oz
50 g	2 oz (2 tbl)	2 oz
75 g	3 oz	3 oz
100 g	4 oz	4 oz
150 g	6 oz	6 oz
200 g	7 oz	7 oz
325 g	12 oz	12 oz
1 litre (10 dl)	1000 ml (2 pints)	3 3/4 cups
1/2 litre (5 dl)	500 ml (1 pint)	1 2/3 cup
1/2 dl	50 ml (3 tbl)	3 tbl
3/4 dl	75 ml (4 1/2 tbl)	4 1/2 tbl
1 dl	100 ml (6 tbl)	1/3 cup
2 dl	200 ml	2/3 cup
2 1/2 dl	250 ml (1/2 pint)	scant cup
3 dl	300 ml	1 cup
4 dl	400 ml	1 1/3 cup
5 dl	500 ml (1 pint)	1 2/3 cup
6 dl	600 ml	2 cups
8 dl	800 ml	2 2/3 cups
	tbl = tablespoon (level)	tbl = tablespoon (level)
	tsp = teaspoon (level)	tsp = teaspoon (level)

Foreword

The Swedish "smörgåsbord" is a national institution which has become known all over the world, and has tempted many to try their hand at Swedish style cooking.

This collection of recipes can be looked upon as a love letter to the ancient cooking traditions of Sweden.

I gathered the material during numerous trips all over the country, and have in my capacity of professional cook personally tested all the recipes. The collection in this book contains both old and new recipes, all examples of true Swedish country cooking.

I hope that this book will inspire gourmets from all over the world to culinary experiments in home cooking.

The illustrations, which are so fitting both from a historical and a cultural standpoint when it comes to the cooking and eating habits of the Swedish people, were made by the artist Ylva Källström-Eklund.

Good luck to all you food-lovers!
OSKAR JAKOBSSON

Contents

Skåne	9	Västmanland	78
Blekinge	21	Dalarna	84
Halland	25	Gästrikland	90
Bohuslän	31	Hälsingland	95
Dalsland	36	Medelpad	99
Småland	39	Härjedalen	102
Öland	44	Jämtland	106
Gotland	48	Ångermanland	110
Östergötland	54	Västerbotten	114
Västergötland	57	Norrbotten	118
Värmland	61	Lappland	124
Närke	66	Map of Sweden	130
Södermanland	69	Index	131
Uppland	74		

skåne

Cabbage Soup from Skåne

4—5 servings

1¼ lbs cabbage
2 carrots
5 small potatoes
6 cups of water or unsalted pork broth
8 allspice berries
salt
3 tablespoons parsley
2 teaspoons butter
½ lb pork or pork sausage

Clean the cabbage and the roots, rinse them with water and cut into 1-inch pieces. Put them in the boiling water or pork broth together with the seasonings and cook covered over low heat until tender. Season the soup to taste with salt. Add the parsley and the butter. Serve with pieces of cooked fresh pork or salted pork or slices of pork sausage.

Pottery Plate Herring

4 servings

2 large Iceland herrings
1 medium size red onion
2 tablespoons dill
1 tablespoon parsley
2 tablespoons butter or margarine

Clean and fillet the herrings, remove skin and all small bones. Soak the fillets in water for 8—12 hours. Serve them on individual plates (preferably earthenware or pottery variety) and garnish with the chopped onion, dill and parsley. Brown the fat and pour over the fillets.

9

Eel Soup

4—5 servings

1½ lbs fresh eel
salt
1 leek
1 carrot
4 allspice berries
3 white peppercorns
2 potatoes
1 tablespoon chopped dill and parsley
2 teaspoons flour
¾ cup milk
1 egg yolk

Clean and skin the eel and cut into 1/2-inch pieces. Cook in lightly salted water until done. Remove and reserve the eel pieces and let the finely chopped vegetables and potatoes cook in the seasoned stock until soft. Stir the flour into the milk and thicken the soup with the flour and milk mixture. Let simmer for 10 minutes. Beat the egg yolk into the soup and add the cooked eel pieces. Sprinkle with the mixture of chopped dill and parsley just before serving.

Black Broth with Giblets

10—12 servings

Stock:
5 quarts water
4 lbs crushed veal bones
½ laurel leaf
3 sprigs of parsley
2 teaspoons salt
10 whole cloves
1 whole ginger
1 whole cinnamon stick
6 allspice berries
8 white peppercorns
1 sprig of thyme
1 large onion
2 carrots
1 leek
1 small celery stalk
2½ cups apple peelings

Giblets:

wings
neck
heart
gizzard } of goose

Broth:
about 4 quarts stock
1 quart goose and pig's blood mixed
2 tablespoons sugar
1 cup flour
1 tablespoon vinegar
2 tablespoons molasses
¼—½ cup red wine
¼—½ cup fortified wine
(¼ cup brandy)
(apple and prune juice)

Cook the stock over low heat for 10 hours. Strain and let cool. Cook the giblets in another saucepan with some of the same kinds of vegetables and seasonings used for the stock. Let the giblets cool in their broth. One hour before starting the black broth, beat the flour into the blood. Let the flour swell in the blood, then strain off lumps. Heat the stock to boiling, carefully stir in the blood mixture and reheat slowly till it starts to simmer. Remove the pot from the fire and add the seasonings again, this time the ground variety. Add the vinegar, molasses, wines, and brandy to taste. To make a thinner broth add apple and prune juice. Strain the broth. This broth tastes even better if prepared one day in advance. When reheating the broth stir continuously to prevent curdling. Serve in hot bowls with giblets, raisin sausage, cooked prunes and apple slices on the side.

Raisin Sausage
10—12 servings

½ cup rice
1 goose liver
1/5 lb calf's liver
2 teaspoons flour
about 2 teaspoons salt
1 teaspoon sugar
1 sausage skin or neck skin of goose
½—1 teaspoon finely ground marjoram
2 cups milk
1 egg
1 teaspoon minced onion sautéed in butter
2 tablespoons raisins
½ teaspoon white pepper

Cook the rice in water and add enough of the milk to make a porridge-like consistency. Let the rice cool, then add the ground liver and the egg, flour, raisins, onions and seasonings. Fry a sample and correct the seasonings if necessary. Fill only 2/3 of the skins to prevent them from breaking during cooking. Bind or sew them up carefully. Put the sausage in cold water, prick it lightly, and simmer for 35—45 minutes. Let cool before cutting into ¼-inch slices.

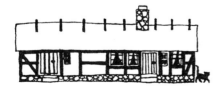

Eel with Curry
4—5 servings

2 lbs fresh eel
1 large onion
10 allspice berries
1 teaspoon salt
2 tablespoons flour
2 tablespoons butter
½ teaspoon curry powder
½ cup cream
1¼ cups stock

Skin and clean the eel and cut into 1-inch pieces. Place the pieces in a pan with water, bring to a boil, skim, and add the salt and the allspice berries. Cook for about 30—40 minutes, remove the eel pieces from the stock and keep warm. Use the stock for making the sauce. Melt the butter, add the flour and the curry powder, stir in the stock. Cook the sauce for 10 minutes. Pour in the cream and correct the seasonings with some more curry powder if necessary. Return the eel pieces to the sauce and serve with cooked rice.

Cooked Salted Eel with Mustard Sauce
4—5 servings

1½—1¾ lbs fresh eel
2/5 lb salt
1 onion
1 small carrot
1 laurel leaf
8 white peppercorns

Clean and skin the eel, split it lengthwise and remove the bones. Cut into serving pieces and rinse in cold water. Cover with the salt and keep in a cool place for 12—15 hours. Rinse off the salt before cooking. Cut the vegetables into thin slices and cook with the eel pieces and the seasonings. Serve with boiled potatoes and mustard sauce.

Mustard Sauce

4 servings

1½ tablespoons butter or margarine
1½ tablespoons flour
1½ cups milk or half-and-half
1—2 tablespoons prepared Skåne mustard
(salt)

Melt the butter and add the flour. Stir in the milk and simmer the mixture for 10 minutes. Season to taste with the mustard and a little salt if desired.

Smoked Eel and Skåne Potatoes

4 servings

1 lb smoked eel

Skåne Potatoes:

8 medium potatoes, boiled or raw
1 large onion
3 tablespoons butter or margarine
2 cups cream
salt
white pepper, ground
soy sauce
chopped parsley

Cut the potatoes into ½-inch cubes and sauté in the butter. Mince the onion and sauté with the potatoes. Add the cream, a little at a time, and simmer with the potatoes for a little while. Add seasonings and enough soy sauce to color the potatoes light brown. Sprinkle with the parsley and serve with the eel (cut into 3-inch pieces). Garnish the eel platter with lettuce leaves, tomato and lemon wedges, and sprigs of dill.
Scrambled eggs with thyme can be substituted for the Skåne Potatoes.

Fresh Eel on Straw

about 2/5 lb eel per serving
1 teaspoon salt
a dash of white pepper
a dash of allspice

Clean and skin a large eel and cut into serving pieces. Cover an oblong baking pan with clean, finely chopped rye straw. Sprinkle salt and freshly ground white pepper and allspice on the eel pieces. Put the pieces on the straw back side up and roast in a hot oven till nicely browned, about 20 minutes. Most of the fat from the eel will run down into the straw during baking. The fumes from the slightly singed straw give a specially delicious flavor to the eel. Serve with lemon wedges, dill sprigs and riced potatoes.

Mock Wild Boar Roast with Morel Sauce

10—12 servings

1 fresh ham
1 turnip
5 shallots
5 red onions
1 laurel leaf
5 whole cloves
2 carrots
1 celery stalk
juice of 1 lemon
1 bottle inexpensive red wine
10 juniper berries, crushed
10 allspice berries
10 white peppercorns
3 tablespoons cooking oil
2 tablespoons wine vinegar

Sauce:

2 quarts fresh morels
3½ cups pan juices
1 cup sour cream
2½ tablespoons butter
2½ tablespoons flour
(salt)
(white pepper)
2 tablespoons butter (for frying)

Cut the rind of the ham in diamond pattern. Cut the vegetables into ½-inch cubes and mix all the ingredients to make a broth. Place the ham in a deep stone jar or other suitable receptacle and pour the broth over it. Let the ham soak for 5—6 days, turning it every day. Roast the ham in the oven, keep covered with paper to prevent the rind from getting too browned. Baste with the broth and additional red wine if desired. Make the sauce from the butter and the flour, the pan juices from the roast and the sour cream. Parboil the morels, sauté in the butter and add to the sauce. Season to taste with additional salt and pepper. Serve the roast with the sauce and browned or mashed potatoes.

Curried Pork from Skåne

5 servings

2 lbs lean side of pork
4 onions
curry to taste
2 teaspoons flour

Cut the pork into ½-inch cubes, mince the onions and brown with the pork. Sprinkle with a teaspoon curry and some salt. Add 1½ cups water and cook for 30—40 minutes. Remove the pork and reserve. Thicken the sauce with a mixture of the flour and ½ a cup of water and cook for 10 minutes. Season to taste with additional curry and salt. Return the pork cubes to the sauce and heat again to boiling point. Serve with boiled or mashed potatoes.

Egg Cake with Smoked Pork

4—5 servings

1 lb smoked pork
2½ cups milk
7 eggs
¾ cup flour
(1 teaspoon sugar)

Slice the pork and brown lightly. Let half of the grease remain in the pan. Beat together the eggs, flour and milk and pour into the warm pan. Cut through the mixture with a spatula during the baking to prevent sticking and burning. When the cake seems firm enough it is turned over onto a suitable pot cover or platter. Return the pork to the pan and add some of the grease, then slide the cake back into the pan. Arrange the cake with the pork side up. Serve with lingonberry sauce.

Stone Cakes with Fried Pork

4 servings

½ lb flour
2½ cups milk
4/5 ounce yeast
1 teaspoon salt
½ teaspoon sugar
about 1 lb salted pork

Mix the flour and the salt in a bowl, warm the milk and add a little at a time. Dissolve the yeast in a mixture of 2 tablespoons warm milk and the sugar, and stir into the flour mixture. Work the batter thoroughly till it becomes elastic and shiny. Cover and let rise in a warm place for 1—2 hours. Bake like pancakes in the grease from the fried pork. Serve with fried pork and lingonberry sauce.

Pork Stew from Skåne

6—8 servings

1 smoked shank of pork
1 salted shank of pork
2 parsnips
1 small celery stalk
¾ cup barley
4 carrots
2 leeks
8 potatoes

Cook the shanks and skim thoroughly. Remove the shanks when done. Cut the vegetables into thick slices and cook in the stock together with the barley. Add the potatoes a little later. Serve the shanks warm with the vegetables.

Roast Goose from Skanör

10—12 servings

1 12-lb goose
2½—3 cups bouillon or water
1—1½ teaspoons arrowroot or potato starch
1½ quarts cooking apples cut in halves
75 prunes
½ lemon
salt
white pepper
applesauce

Clean out, rinse and wipe the goose. Rub it thoroughly inside and out first with lemon then with salt and pepper. Fill it with the prunes and the apples, sew it up and bind with strong cord. Roast in warm oven (about 450°F).

After 10 minutes add enough water or bouillon to cover the bottom of the pan. Baste often with pan juices. Add more liquids after a while. If the goose is browning too quickly cover it with buttered paper. Allow about 10 minutes of roasting per pound.

Towards the end of the roasting time pour some cold water over the skin to make it crisp and shiny. Leave the oven door slightly open during the last 8—10 minutes; this will give extra crispness to the skin. Prick the goose with a fork or a skewer to test doneness, the bird is done when the escaping liquid is colorless. Place the goose on a serving platter, pour the pan juices into a saucepan and skim thoroughly.

Let the juices come to a boil, then thicken with arrowroot or potato starch that has been dissolved in a few tablespoons of cold water. Season to taste with salt, pepper and some applesauce. After the goose has cooled remove the cord and the stuffing. Slice carefully and put slices back into the shape of the goose. (For this you will need a very sharp carving knife.) Serve the goose on a large platter decorated with slices of cooked apples and prunes, serve with red cabbage (see recipe below), applesauce and boiled or browned potatoes.

Cured Goose with Horseradish Cream or Wine Sauce

10—12 servings

1 12-lb goose
½ lemon
1½ cups salt
1½ cups sugar
½ teaspoon potassium nitrate (saltpeter)
3 quarts water
6 white peppercorns
1 onion
1 carrot
3 sprigs parsley
1 laurel leaf

Sauce:

3½ cups stock
1 cup red wine
arrowroot
soy sauce
salt

Brine:

about 3 quarts water
1 cup salt
½ cup sugar

Horseradish Cream:

2 cups cream
1—2 tablespoons grated horseradish

Pluck, draw and wash the goose. Rub it with the lemon and a mixture of the salt, saltpeter and sugar and keep in a cool place for 24 hours. Cook a brine with 1 cup salt and ½ cup sugar. Let the brine cool, then immerse the goose and keep in a cold place for 3 days. Truss the bird and cook over low heat with the seasonings and the vegetables for about 2 hours. Skim thoroughly. Cut and slice the goose and serve with whipped cream mixed with freshly grated horseradish. The cream should be chilled. Or serve with a warm wine sauce, made of stock and red wine, thickened and lightly colored with soy sauce. Cured goose can also be served cold with red cabbage, mashed potatoes and horseradish cream.

Red Cabbage

10—12 servings

1 large head red cabbage
3 apples
⅓ cup margarine or goose fat
1 large onion
1 bacon rind
1½—2 cups water
2 tablespoons molasses
1 tablespoon vinegar
2 teaspoons salt
½ teaspoon white pepper

Melt the fat in a Dutch oven. Add the shredded cabbage and the sliced onion and brown lightly. Add peeled apple wedges, the bacon rind and some of the water. Simmer covered until the cabbage is tender. Add more water occasionally. Season carefully with the seasonings and the molasses. The dish should have a mild and pleasant sour-sweet taste. Cooking time 1½—2 hours.

Beef Stew from Skåne
5 servings

2 lbs brisket of beef
2 large carrots
2 large onions
2 tablespoons flour
salt
white pepper (ground)
10 allspice berries
1 laurel leaf
2 tablespoons fat or oil

Cut the meat (do not remove the bones) into ½—1 inch cubes. Salt and pepper and brown quickly in very hot fat. Cut the onions and the carrots into large pieces and brown with the meat. Transfer meat and vegetables to a Dutch oven or saucepan and stir in the flour. Add some warm water and the seasonings. Bring to boiling point, skim thoroughly and continue to simmer under cover. Cook until the meat can easily be separated from the bones. Do not strain the stew. Serve with boiled potatoes and red beets. This type of stew should always be served piping hot.

Roast Venison
4—5 servings

3 lbs venison roast
1/5 lb bacon for larding
3 tablespoons cooking oil
1/5 lb butter or margarine
1½ tablespoons flour
1 onion
1 carrot
5 juniper berries (crushed)
1½ cups cream or half-and-half
salt
white pepper

Wash and dry the meat. Cut the bacon into thin strips and lard the meat. Salt and pepper the meat on all sides and brown it in the oil, using a large saucepan or Dutch oven. Baste and turn the roast several times during cooking. Add the onion and the crushed juniper berries. Remove the roast when done, reduce the sauce to about half by cooking, and strain. Make a gravy with the butter, flour, sauce and cream. Season to taste. Slice the roast. Serve with rowan-berry or cranberry jelly and potatoes browned in butter.

Crullers
45 cookies

3 egg yolks
3 tablespoons sugar
3 tablespoons light cream
2 cups flour
1½ tablespoons butter or margarine
½ tablespoon grated lemon peel
1½ tablespoons brandy

Stir the butter and the sugar and add the remaining ingredients, ending with the flour. Let the dough rest in a cool place for about 3 hours. Roll the dough to the thickness of a penny. Cut pieces 3 inches long and ¼ inch wide with a pastry wheel. Make a ¾ inch slit in the middle of each piece and pull one end through the slit. Cook the crullers golden brown in oil or good quality frying fat (350°—360°F). Remove from the oil, place on paper, and sprinkle with a little sugar.

Yeast Pancakes
5—6 servings

5 eggs
2½ cups milk
2—2½ cups flour
1 teaspoon cardamom
2 tablespoons melted butter
2 tablespoons sugar
1 teaspoon salt
1 ounce yeast

Beat the eggs with 1½ cups of the milk and add the flour, melted butter, ground cardamom, sugar, salt and yeast. Let the batter rise for about 1 hour, then add the rest of the milk. Bake the cakes in a special griddle for small pancakes or in a frying pan. Serve with jam.

Good Old Spitcake

15—20 servings

Ever since the 18th century this has been the traditional wedding cake in Skåne. It lends a very festive atmosphere to all kinds of celebrations and get-togethers.

20 egg yolks
4/5 lb confectioners' sugar
3/5 lb flour
1/5 potato starch
a few drops of lemon oil

Beat together the yolks and the sugar and add the flour. Bind a white paper around a rotating spit, to which a coni-cal shape made of wood or metal has been fastened. Butter the paper. Place the spit over an even fire, preferably of beech-wood embers. Pour some of the batter into a pitcher, and while the spit is slowly rotated let the batter very, very slowly coil down onto the conical shape on the spit. The layers of coiled batter should be so thin that they get baked during one turn of the spit. When almost all the batter is used up, pull the spit in uneven jerks to make little tips stick out from the cake. Finally a sugar frosting is dripped onto the tips of the cake or swirled between them. For extra effect sprinkle colored sugar over the cake before the frosting has hardened.

BLEKINGE

Clear Fish Soup

4—5 servings

2 leeks
5 tomatoes
3 tablespoons chopped parsley
1½ quarts water
juice from 3 lemons
½ lb cod fillets
1 tablespoon butter
salt
white pepper
white bread

Clean the leeks, cut them into inch-long strips (leaving out the green parts). Scald and peel the tomatoes. Cut them in half and squeeze out the seeds. Cut into smaller pieces. Cut the cod fillets into inch-long pieces. Fry the leeks in the butter, add the fish, tomatoes and parsley. Add cold water and a little salt and cook for 20 minutes. Season to taste with the lemon juice and the salt. Serve the soup with croutons.

Eel Soup

4—5 servings

1½ lbs lightly salted eel
3 white peppercorns
3 allspice berries
1 large carrot
2 leeks
1 parsnip
1 small celery stalk
5—6 potatoes
a pinch of pepper
(salt)
1 tablespoon dill
1 tablespoon parsley

Cut the eel into inch-thick slices and cook in salted water with the seasonings. Chop the vegetables finely and add to the soup. Skim thoroughly. After 10 minutes add the potatoes, cut into ¼-inch cubes. Continue to cook the soup covered until done, season to taste with the white pepper and some salt if desired. Finally sprinkle the minced dill and parsley over the soup before serving.

Bread Soup

6 servings

3/5 lb bread
30 prunes
1/5 lb raisins
red currant juice to taste
sugar to taste
1½ quarts water

In a large family there is often left-over pieces of bread. Place these, preferably sour dough rye bread, in water in a stone jar or other suitable receptacle. After 5—6 days the bread has turned sour. Beat it and let it come

to a boil in a saucepan. Add the cooked prunes and the raisins. If the bread is not sour enough you can add some red currant juice. The soup is then seasoned to taste with sugar.

Broiled Salted Eel

4 servings

2/5 lb eel per serving
4 tablespoons salt
4 tablespoons butter
2 tablespoons dill
2 tablespoons flour
1 tablespoon oil
8 medium potatoes
1½ cups milk or half-and-half

Clean, skin and split the eel lengthwise. Remove the center bone. Salt the eel for 24 hours. Rinse quickly before broiling. Cut the eel into 4-inch pieces and brush with the oil. Broil it directly on the stove or in a dry frying pan. Serve the eel with dill butter and creamed potatoes or with scrambled eggs.

Oldfashioned Fried Salmon

4 servings

4 slices salmon, each ¼—⅓ lb
2 teaspoons salt
1 teaspoon pepper
4 teaspoons oil
1 cup bread crumbs
4 eggs
8 sprigs of parsley
5 tablespoons butter
1 tablespoon anchovy sauce

Salt and pepper the salmon slices and put aside for 7—8 minutes. Turn them over in a little oil and then in the bread crumbs, heat a small amount of oil in a frying pan and fry the salmon over low heat. Serve with poached eggs, frizzled parsley and a sauce made of melted butter seasoned with anchovy sauce.

Creamed Dried Codfish

4 servings

¼ lb dried codfish per serving
1½ cups cream
2 tablespoons butter
2 tablespoons flour

Cut the fish into pieces, remove all bones and skin. Soak in water for 1½ —2 days, then boil for 45 minutes. If the broth is too salty it is poured off and fresh water is used for cooking the fish. Chop the fish into small pieces and cream it in a white cream sauce. Serve with cooked rice or riced potatoes.

Dried Cod Pudding

6—7 servings

3/5 lb cooked dried cod, skinned and boned
¾ cup rice
3—3½ cups milk
½ quart water
2 eggs
1/5 lb margarine
salt
white pepper

Rinse the rice under cold water, cook it first in water then in milk a little at a time, till it has reached a consistency of thin porridge. Let it cool slightly. Beat the eggs and stir into the porridge. Season with salt and white pepper. Cut the fish into ½-inch pieces and add to the rice. Pour the mixture into a greased baking dish and bake at 450°F for about 30 minutes. Serve with melted butter.

23

Cherry Pancakes

To make an ordinary Swedish pancake batter mix together 1 cup flour, 2 tablespoons sugar and ¼ teaspoon salt, then add 3 eggs mixed with 3 cups milk. Grease the pan with butter and heat, fill the pan sections with batter. Immediately place 4 fresh, pitted and sweetened cherries on each pancake. Turn and bake till golden brown on both sides. Sprinkle with sugar and serve immediately.

Sugar Cakes

5 eggs
2/5 lb confectioners' sugar
2/5 lb flour

Beat together the eggs and the sugar for 15 minutes. Stir in the flour. Drop the batter from a spoon onto a greased cookie sheet and bake in a medium hot oven till light yellow in color.

24

Salmon Soup

5 servings

Stock:
head and bone of one salmon
1 onion
1 leek (only the white part)
1 large carrot
5 dill stems
5 parsley stems
4 white peppercorns
4 allspice berries
salt

Soup:
1 tablespoon butter
1 tablespoon flour
1 quart stock
½ cup cream
2 egg yolks
4 tablespoons cooked carrots cut into small cubes
4 tablespoons small green peas, cooked
2 tablespoons each minced parsley and dill
(salt)
(white pepper)

Remove the gills from the salmon head, then cut the head and the center bone into smaller pieces. Rinse them quickly in cold water. Put them in cold water in a saucepan and bring to a boil. Skim thoroughly, chop the vegetables and add to the stock with the seasonings and some salt. Cook over low heat for about 45 minutes. Strain the stock. To make soup heat the butter, stir in the flour until blended, add the stock and cook over low heat for 15 minutes. Beat together the egg yolks and the cream and stir into the soup. Season to taste with salt and white pepper. Add the cooked vegetables, parsley and dill. If there is still some salmon meat left on the head and the center bone, mince it and stir into the soup.

Cod Stew from Falkenberg

6 servings

3 small codfish
6 tomatoes
about ¾ cup chopped parsley
6 tablespoons butter

Brine:

about 1 quart water
6 dill stems
3   small carrots, sliced
juice from ½ lemon
salt
1 onion, sliced
6 white peppercorns
1 laurel leaf

Clean and rinse the codfish and cut into pieces. Prepare brine and cook covered over low heat for 20—25 minutes. Add the fish and cook slowly until done. Add the tomatoes, cut into wedges, the butter and the parsley. Season to taste with a little salt. Serve with steaming hot boiled potatoes.

Fried Cod Roe

4 servings

roe from 2 large codfish
2 tablespoons flour
3 tablespoons butter or margarine
2 teaspoons salt
½ teaspoon white pepper
1 lemon
1 tablespoon minced dill

Rinse the roe carefully, wind it up in a piece of thin linen material and tie with a thin cord. Put in cold, salted water, bring to a boil and cook over low heat for 25—30 minutes, depending on the size of the roe. Remove the roe and press lightly between two cutting boards. When cooled cut roe into slices at an angle. Turn the slices over in some flour, season and fry quickly in the butter. Put on a hot serving platter, pour the butter over and sprinkle with the dill. Garnish with lemon wedges. Serve with boiled or riced potatoes.

Broiled Turbot Fillets with Horse-radish Mayonnaise

4—5 servings

2 lbs turbot fillets
1 tablespoon oil
salt
white pepper
2 tablespoons dill
1 cup mayonnaise
about 2 teaspoons horse-radish
(2 tablespoons whipped cream)

Season the fillets and brush them with a small amount of oil. Broil directly on the stove or in a dry frying pan. Put on a serving platter and sprinkle with the minced dill. Stir the freshly grated horse-radish into the mayonnaise, add whipped cream if desired. Serve with boiled potatoes.

Steamed Smoked Eel with Scrambled Eggs and Chives

4—5 servings

1 lb smoked eel
2 tablespoons minced chives
4—5 dill sprigs
(1 lemon)

Cut the eel into serving pieces. Steam for 8—10 minutes in a double boiler. Serve on top of a layer of scrambled eggs seasoned with the minced chives. Garnish with dill sprigs and lemon wedges if desired.

Boiled Salmon with Cream Sauce

7—8 servings

2 lbs salmon

Trimming:
1 lemon
5 dill sprigs

Brine:
1 quart water
4—5 dill stems
1 tablespoon salt
6 white peppercorns
1 onion
1 leek
1 carrot
2 teaspoons vinegar

Sauce:
2 tablespoons butter
2 tablespoons flour
1½ cups fish broth
1 cup cream
the juice of one lemon

Clean the salmon and wipe with a cloth. Mix the brine and boil covered for 20—30 minutes. Add the fish and cook very slowly. Put on a serving platter when done and garnish with lemon slices or wedges and plenty of dill sprigs. Make the sauce by melting the butter, stirring in the flour and diluting with equal parts of broth and cream. Season with the lemon juice.

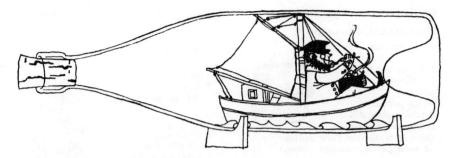

Salmon Pudding from Halland
4—5 servings

½ lb lightly salted salmon
3 tablespoons minced dill
2 eggs
¼—½ cup cream
3 tablespoons minced onion
½ teaspoon white pepper
1 teaspoon sugar
(salt)
1½ lbs boiled potatoes, peeled
butter

Cut the salmon into small cubes and fry quickly in butter together with the onion. Add the dill. Rice the freshly boiled potatoes, mix with the eggs and the cream, then with the salmon mixture. Season to taste with white pepper, salt and sugar (go light on the salt). Pour the mixture into a greased and floured mold. Sprinkle the surface with bread crumbs and dots of butter. Bake for 30—40 minutes in hot oven (480°F). Serve with melted butter.

Sailor's Steak
4 servings

4 slices round or flank steak, about 1/8 inch thick, weighing about ¼ lb each
½ laurel leaf
salt
white pepper
2 large onions, sliced
10—12 potatoes, sliced
6 white peppercorns
3 allspice berries
4 tablespoons margarine
about ½ quart bouillon or water
(1 bottle beer)

Salt and pepper the steaks, then fry quickly in a hot frying pan. Sauté the sliced onions. Alternate layers of potatoes, onions, steaks and potatoes in a saucepan. Rinse out the frying pan with some water and add to saucepan. Add the seasonings, bouillon or water (or a bottle of beer). Cook covered till the steaks feel quite tender. This dish should be served piping hot, directly from the pan.

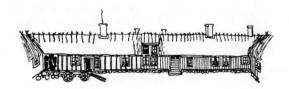

Lamb Stew

5 servings

2 lbs breast or shoulder of lamb
1½ lbs potatoes, peeled
2 onions
1 leek
2 carrots
1 celery stalk
2 teaspoons salt
5 white peppercorns
2 tablespoons chopped parsley

Cut the meat into inch-size cubes, parboil it and rinse with running cold water till water is perfectly clear. Place in fresh water with the cubed vegetables. Bring to a boil and skim thoroughly. Add the seasonings, and when the meat is almost done add the cubed potatoes. Season to taste with more salt if necessary. Sprinkle with the chopped parsley and serve directly from the pan.

Venison Meat Loaf with Morel Sauce

4 servings

4/5 lb ground venison meat
½ cup bread crumbs
2 eggs
1—1½ cups cream or half-and-half
1 tablespoon oil (for frying)
1 tablespoon margarine (for frying)
salt
white pepper

Grind the meat twice. Soak the breadcrumbs in the cream or the half-and-half. Put the meat in a bowl, add the salt, pepper and eggs, then the bread crumbs. Add more cream until the meat mixture reaches the desired consistency. Season and fry a sample. Shape and bake like ordinary meat loaf.

Sauce:
1 quart fresh morels
4 teaspoons butter
4 teaspoons flour
1 cup cream
salt
white pepper
½ cup water or bouillon

Rinse the morels thoroughly several times. Cut into large pieces and sauté in butter. Sprinkle with the flour and add the cream. When meat loaf is done, remove it from the pan, add the water or the bouillon to the pan and bring to a boil while stirring. Reduce to about half by cooking, strain and add to morel sauce. Season to taste. Serve the meat loaf with fried, boiled or mashed potatoes.

Scrambled Eggs Country Style

4 servings

1 tablespoon butter
2 tablespoons flour
2½ cups milk
6 eggs
1 teaspoon salt
a pinch of pepper

Heat the butter in a pan, stir in the flour until blended, add the milk. Cook over low heat for 10 minutes. Carefully beat the eggs into the sauce. Season with the salt and the white pepper. Serve with fried bacon or sausages.

Spinach Pancakes

4 servings

2/5 lb frozen spinach
4 tablespoons butter or margarine
2 eggs
1½ cups flour
2½ cups milk
½ teaspoon salt
sugar

Thaw the spinach and mix into a thick batter made of the rest of the ingredients. If fresh spinach leaves are being used they have to be parboiled and cut into thin strips before mixing into the pancake batter. Make ordinary Swedish pancakes in a special pancake griddle. Serve them with browned butter.

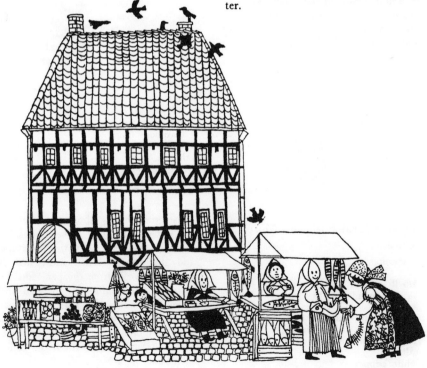

BOHUSLÄN

Mussel Soup

4 servings

30 fresh mussels (live, common sea mussel)
1 onion
1 leek (the white part only)
1 small celery stalk
2 tablespoons parsley
4 potatoes
4 cups water
½ lemon
½ cup cream
2 tablespoons butter or margarine
salt
white pepper

Scrub and brush the mussels carefully and rinse. (If some mussels have opened and do not close immediately after a light tap on the shell, these must be discarded as inedible.) Chop the vegetables finely, sauté in butter in a saucepan, add the water and the lemon juice and bring to a boil. Add the mussels and boil them quickly under cover. Remove the mussels after a few minutes and add the potatoes cut into small cubes. While the soup is continuing to boil, remove the mussels from the shells and clean them. Finally add the cream and the parsley to the soup and season to taste with salt and pepper. Put the mussels back in the soup and serve it very hot.

Sea Crayfish Soup

4 servings

4 sea crayfish, live
4 cups water
¼ can fishballs
2 tablespoons dill
2 tablespoons butter or margarine
1½ tablespoons flour
¾ cup light cream
½ bouillon cube
salt
white pepper

Boil the crayfish for about 20 minutes in lightly salted water. Clean the crayfish and cut the tails into several smaller pieces. Cut the fishballs into four parts and put in a saucepan with the crayfish tails, the entrails, and the minced dill. Add the boiling stock and the bouillon cube. Make a ball of the butter, flour and cream, if it tends to become too hard dilute with some of the stock. Check the saltiness of the soup before seasoning the batter ball. Take small pieces of the ball with a teaspoon and add to the soup, then cook for 10 minutes. Serve the soup very hot.

Shrimp au Gratin

4 servings

4/5 lb fresh shrimp
1 large apple
2 teaspoons minced chives
½ teaspoon curry
1 teaspoon ketchup
1 tablespoon butter
1 tablespoon flour
2½ cups half-and-half
salt
1 egg yolk
2 tablespoons grated cheese

Creamed Crab

1 serving

1 medium female crab
1 tablespoon butter
2 teaspoons flour
1 egg yolk
½ cup half-and-half
1 anchovy fillet
1 lemon wedge
2 teaspoons chopped dill
cayenne pepper
salt
1 dill sprig

Clean the shrimp and chop them lightly. Peel the apple and cut into cubes. Sauté the shrimp and the curry in the butter, sprinkle with the flour and add the half-and-half. Let the sauce cook for 5 minutes, add the ketchup, the cubed apple and the chives. Season to taste with salt and some white pepper if desired. Stir in the yolk and bring to a boil for a moment. Pour into a mould, sprinkle with the cheese and bake near to the top of a hot oven. Serve with mashed or boiled potatoes, or with rice topped with a pat of butter.

Remove all the crab meat from the shell and cut into small cubes. Make a white sauce from the butter, flour and half-and-half. Add the yolk and season with chopped anchovy, lemon, a pinch of cayenne pepper and some salt if desired. Finally add the dill and the crab meat. Season carefully. Pour the creamed crab back into the shell and garnish with a pretty dill sprig or with the roe.

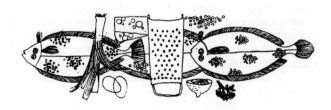

Ovenbaked Sole

4 servings

3 medium sole
2 tablespoons butter or margarine
1 leek
1 tablespoon chopped parsley
the juice of ½ lemon
1 cup cream
2 teaspoons beurre manié (equal parts of cold butter and flour kneaded into a ball)
2 egg yolks
1 tablespoon grated cheese
salt
white pepper

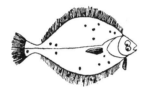

Skin and fillet the fish and rinse quickly in cold water. Grease a large, not too high saucepan. Cut the white part of the leek into small cubes and put in the bottom of the pan. Place the fillets on top of the cubed leek. Cover the fish with water, add the lemon juice and cover with greased paper or a pot cover. Remove fish when done. Boil the stock a while to reduce it slightly, then add the cream, and thicken the sauce by adding parts of the beurre manié. Simmer for 5 minutes. Beat in the egg yolks, add the parsley and season. Place the fillets in a greased, oven-proof pan. Pour the sauce over the fish to cover it completely. Sprinkle with the cheese and bake in oven till golden brown. Serve with boiled potatoes.

Boiled Plaice Fillets with Morel Sauce

4 servings

4 medium plaice
2½—3½ cups fresh morels
4 teaspoons butter or margarine
2½ cups cream or half-and-half
½ lemon
1 tablespoon flour
salt
white pepper

Clean, fillet and rinse the fish. Grease the bottom of the saucepan and add the fillets. Add the salt and the lemon juice and cover the fish with water. Cook covered over low heat. Sauté the chopped morels in the butter, add flour and cream and dilute with the fish stock if necessary. Season with salt and pepper. Place the fish on a serving dish and pour the sauce over it. Serve with riced potatoes or boiled new potatoes or rice.

Pickled Mackerel

6 servings

3 lbs mackerel
3 tablespoons salt
3 tablespoons sugar
2 teaspoons white pepper
¾ cup dill, chopped

Clean, fillet and rinse the fish. Drain it and wipe with a towel. Mix salt, sugar and the coursely ground pepper. Alternate layers of fish, pickling mixture, and dill in a suitable bowl. Let the fillets rest with the meaty parts towards each other. Place a plate weighted down with some heavy object on top of the fish and keep in a cool place for at least 24 hours. Serve with Mustard sauce (page 126) and boiled potatoes with dill.

Boiled Mackerel with Gooseberry Sauce

4 servings

4 medium mackerels
salt
white pepper
1 tablespoon vinegar
1 tablespoon butter or margarine
2 teaspoons sugar
2½ cups gooseberries (half ripe)
nutmeg

Clean the fish and cut off heads and tails. Rinse thoroughly and boil in water with the salt and the vinegar. Cut the stems off the gooseberries and rinse. Boil the berries in 1½ cups water. Drain and pass the berries through a sieve. Add the butter, sugar, salt, a small amount of grated nutmeg and white pepper and heat the sauce. Season carefully; the sauce should have a fresh, sour-sweet taste.

Stuffed Whiting Fillets

4 servings

8 small whitings
1 large onion
2 tablespoons parsley
1 teaspoon thyme
flour
2 eggs
bread crumbs
salt
white pepper
butter or margarine
1 lemon

Clean and fillet the fish. Salt and pepper the fillets and place them two and two together with a filling of minced onion, parsley and thyme between each pair. Dip first in flour, then in lightly beaten eggs, then bread crumbs. Fry in plenty of butter and place on a serving platter. Sprinkle with chopped parsley and garnish with lemon wedges. Serve with riced or mashed potatoes.

Deep-Fat Fried Apple Rings

15 rings

1 egg
¼ cup milk
½ cup flour
1 teaspoon baking powder
a pinch of salt
15 raw apple rings (¼ inch thick)
5 teaspoons cinnamon
2 teaspoons confectioners' sugar
about ½ quart oil or cooking fat

Beat together the egg and the milk and add the flour, salt and baking powder. Heat the oil or cooking fat. Sprinkle the rings with the cinnamon, dip them in the batter and cook them in the oil till golden brown and crisp. Remove with a perforated ladle or a fork and place on a paper towel. Sift the confectioners' sugar over the rings and serve them warm with jelly or jam and cold whipped cream or light cream.

Jelly Roll

15 slices

2 eggs
2 teaspoons melted butter
⅓ lb sugar
2.6 ounces flour
1.6 ounces potato starch
¼ cup hot water
1 teaspoon baking powder

Filling:
¾—1 cup raspberry jam mixed with applesauce

Garnish:
1 cup heavy cream
4 teaspoons raspberry jam

Beat the eggs and the sugar till light, add the hot water and beat for another minute or two. Mix together the flour and the baking powder, sift into the batter while stirring constantly. Grease a piece of wax paper, 12" × 12". Place on a cookie sheet. Spread the batter on the paper and bake in the oven at about 480°F, till golden brown, about 4—6 minutes. Turn the cake over onto another paper sprinkled with sugar. Carefully remove the first paper. Spread the filling on the cake and roll it up immediately. Remove the paper when the cake is cool. Place on a serving platter and trim off the edges evenly. Whip the cream and spread evenly over the entire roll. Finally garnish with small dots of the jam.

DALSLAND

Chicken Soup

4—5 servings

1 chicken
6 medium potatoes
1 large red onion
a pinch of white pepper
2 teaspoons vinegar
1 teaspoon sugar
1 teaspoon salt
2 tablespoons parsley

Clean and rinse the chicken, place in cold water and slowly bring to a boil. Skim thoroughly and simmer under cover. Remove the chicken when done, cut the potatoes into pieces, mince the onion and let potatoes and onion cook in the chicken stock until the potatoes fall apart. Beat the soup till it is smooth and season to taste with the vinegar, salt, sugar and white pepper. Add the chicken meat, cut into cubes or strips. Do not let the soup get too thick. Sprinkle the chopped parsley over the soup when serving.

Fancy Pike Perch

4 servings

2 small pike perches
salt
pepper
¾ cup light cream
2½ tablespoons margarine or butter
2 tablespoons chopped red beets mixed
   with 1 teaspoon minced chives
1 tablespoon parsley

Clean, rinse and fillet the fish. Salt
and pepper the fillets and fry until gold-
en brown. Add the cream. Remove
the fish and place on a serving platter.
Sprinkle with the red beets, chives
and parsley, then pour the boiling
cream over. Serve with boiled potatoes
with dill.

Boiled Salted Spareribs with Parsley Sauce

4 servings

2 lbs salted spareribs
about 1 quart water
4 white peppercorns
4 allspice berries
½ laurel leaf
1 leek

Sauce:
1½ cups stock
1 tablespoon (or more) chopped parsley
1 tablespoon butter
1 tablespoon flour

Cook the ribs together with the seasonings and the sliced leek. Skim
thoroughly. When making the sauce
heat the butter, stir in the flour and
add the stock. Add plenty of chopped
parsley. Cut the ribs up and serve in
the sauce with mashed potatoes.

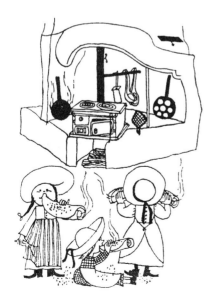

Griddle Cake with Oatmeal and Apples

6 servings

2.4 ounces butter or margarine
2.4 ounces sugar (for batter)
3 tablespoons milk
1 teaspoon baking powder
2½ cups oatmeal
1½ lbs hard apples
2.4 ounces sugar (for apples)

Peel the apples, cut them into thin wedges and cook them in small amount of water and 2.4 ounces of sugar. Knead together the rest of the ingredients and roll out to make four layers. Bake these, then stack them with a layer of the compote between them. Finish with a layer of the compote on top. Serve the cake with whipped cream, light cream or custard.

Vanilla Pancakes

4 servings

2½ cups ordinary pancake batter (page 24)
8 tablespoons applesauce
2 tablespoons vanilla sugar
butter or margarine
1 cup heavy cream

Bake the pancakes very thin. Fill them with the applesauce and roll each one into a little package. Place the pancakes on an ovenproof platter and sift the vanilla sugar over them. Right before serving put the platter in a warm oven (480°F) for about 5 minutes. Figure on two pancakes per person and serve with whipped cream.

Apple Cake from Åmål

4 servings

6 large apples
½ cup peeled and chopped sweet almonds
½ cup sugar
1—3 tablespoons milk
3 tablespoons butter
1 tablespoon flour

Peel the apples and cut into large wedges. Cook them for 2 minutes in water and sugar, then place them on a greased ovenproof platter. Quickly boil the butter, flour and milk in a saucepan and add the almond and the sugar. Cover the apples with the batter and bake in the oven at about 440°F until light golden in color. Serve warm with whipped or light cream.

SMÅLAND

Crayfish Soup

6—7 servings

25 live crayfish
2 minced onions
2 minced carrots
2½ tablespoons butter
2½ tablespoons flour
2½ cups beef bouillon
2½ cups calf bouillon
1 cup white wine
1 cup brandy, madeira or sherry
½ laurel leaf
5 white peppercorns
salt
a pinch of thyme
½ cup heavy cream
1 tablespoon cold butter

Sauté the onions and the carrots in butter in a saucepan. Rinse the crayfish thoroughly and add to onions and carrots, heat covered for 2—3 minutes. Add the seasonings, wine, bouillon and brandy. Cook for 8—10 minutes, then remove the crayfish. Cook the soup for another 10 minutes, then strain through a colander. Melt the butter and add the flour in another saucepan.

Add the soup and bring to a boil. Skim thoroughly and cook for another 10 minutes or so. Add the cream and season to taste. Strain and stir in the cold butter. Shell the crayfish tails, cut them in two and add them to the soup, which should be kept hot till ready to serve. According to taste and economical circumstances the flavor of the soup can be further enhanced by additional amounts of brandy or wine.

Hunting Soup

4 servings

front part of a large hare
3 tablespoons margarine or butter
2 tablespoons flour
1 onion
1 carrot
1 small celery stalk
1 teaspoon salt
½ teaspoon white pepper
½ teaspoon thyme
1 tablespoon red currant jelly
1 cup cream
¼ cup madeira
1½ quarts water
1 bouillon cube

Cut the front part of a hare into small pieces, season and brown in a heavy kettle together with the onion, celery and carrots. Sprinkle with the flour, add the seasonings and the bouillon or water. Bring to a boil and skim thoroughly. Cook the soup until the meat comes off the bones, strain. Scrape the meat off the bones, cut into small pieces and return to the soup. Add the cream and season to taste with the currant jelly and more salt and pepper if desired.

Hunter's Stew

5—6 servings

2 lbs boneless moose meat
4 cups half-and-half
5 cups chanterelle mushrooms
3 onions
2 carrots
3 tablespoons margarine
salt
white pepper
1 teaspoon ground mustard
2 tablespoons red currant jelly

Cut the meat as for collops, season and brown it and place in a saucepan. Sauté the chopped carrots and onions and add to the saucepan. Add water and cook covered over low heat. Remove the meat and the vegetables when they are tender. Reduce the stock to one third by boiling, add the half-and-half and let boil slowly. Season with the mustard and the currant jelly. Return the meat to the gravy. Chop and sauté the chanterelles and add to the gravy. Season to taste. Serve the stew with mashed potatoes.

Ragout of Hare

5—6 servings

1 hare, skinned and cleaned
2 onions
2 carrots
½ teaspoon thyme
5 crushed juniper berries
¼ laurel leaf
2 tablespoons flour
salt
white pepper
3 tablespoons cooking oil
(½ cup cream)

Cut the hare into equal parts about as for collops. Season and sauté quickly in the oil in a heavy kettle together with the onions and the carrots. Add the seasonings and sprinkle with some flour. Add water and bring to a boil, skim thoroughly. Continue to cook and remove the pieces as they get done. Season the gravy to taste and strain, add to the meat and cook for another 7—8 minutes. Serve with rowan-berry jelly or pickled cucumbers and with boiled or mashed potatoes. If desired you can add ½ cup cream to the gravy.

Lamb Chops from Kalmar

4 servings

4 lamb chops
4 slices smoked ham
2 cups parboiled potatoes, cubed
2 tablespoons minced onions, sautéed in butter
2 cups cream
cucumber
parsley
salt
white pepper

Fry the potatoes and the onions and mix them in a saucepan. Add the cream and bring slowly to a boil. Season. Fry the chops and the ham slices. Place in individual serving bowls, if possible, starting with the potatoes, then the lamb chop and finally the ham slice. Garnish with two thin slices of cucumber, and sprinkle with chopped parsley.

Pancake from Småland

3—4 servings

4/5 lb potatoes
4/5 lb carrots
3 egg yolks
2.6 ounces margarine (for the frying pan)
salt
6—8 slices lightly salted pork

Peel the carrots and the potatoes and boil them in a small amount of water with some salt. Grind them in a meat grinder. Stir in the egg yolks, pour the mixture into a greased frying pan, and bake in the oven. After a while turn the pancake over into another pan to let it get browned on both sides. Serve with crisp fried pork slices.

Potato Dumplings ("kroppkakor")

4 servings

10 medium potatoes, peeled
2—3 egg yolks
1—1½ cups flour
1 teaspoon salt
2/5 lb salted pork
2 teaspoons coarsely ground allspice
1 onion, minced
1½ teaspoons salt per quart water (for cooking)

Pass the boiled potatoes through a potato ricer and add the egg yolks and the salt. Let cool, then mix with the flour. Shape this dough into a roll. Cut the pork into ¼-inch cubes and mince the onion. Fry the pork quickly with the onion and add the allspice. Cut the potato roll into inch thick slices, make a hole in each slice and fill with the pork mixture. Cover the hole so that the ham mixture will be in the middle of the slice, shape into round dumplings. Make them perfectly smooth with no fingerprints. Cook the dumplings slowly in plenty of water, uncovered. Cook for 5—6 minutes after the dumplings have floated to the surface. Serve them boiled or fried with melted butter and lingonberry jam (mixed with some cream).

Curd Cake from Småland (Bodafors)

15—20 servings

13—14 quarts milk
8 eggs
4/5 lb sugar
1½ cups flour
3½ cups heavy cream
2 tablespoons rennet
40 sweet almonds
5 bitter almonds

Heat the milk to 90°F. Beat in the flour and add the rennet. Stir the mixture till thickened. Let stand until it has turned to curds and whey. Stir a couple of times to make the curds separate from the whey. Put in a strainer and let the whey run through. Beat the cream, sugar, eggs and the chopped almonds into the curds. Pour the mixture into two greased baking dishes (the tinned copper variety if desired) and bake in the oven at about 350°F, preferably in a waterbath, for 1½—2 hours, or until set and light brown. It is possible to bake the cake without a water-bath, but the result is said to be better with it. Serve the cake right in the baking dish with whipped cream or cinnamon sauce. Strawberry, raspberry, and cherry jam or a mixture of blueberry and raspberry jam are also supposed to be delicious with this cake.

Cinnamon Sauce (for Curd Cake)
15—20 servings

2 tablespoons butter
2 tablespoons flour
6 cups cream
5 egg yolks
2 tablespoons sugar
1—2 teaspoons cinnamon
(sweet almonds)

Beat together a suitable amount of sauce from the butter, flour and cream and cook in a saucepan for 10 minutes. Add the egg yolks, but be careful that the sauce does not come to a boil again. Season to taste with sugar and ground cinnamon, and some minced almonds if desired.

Cream Puffs
12—15 cakes

3 tablespoons melted butter
2½ cups heavy cream
7 tablespoons flour
butter (to grease the pan)

Whip the cream till stiff. Sift the flour into the cream and stir in the melted butter slowly. If the batter is too thick add a few teaspoons of water. Bake the puffs on top of the stove in a special pan. Place them on a serving platter and sprinkle with confectioners' sugar. Serve with cloudberry, raspberry or strawberry jam.

Heart's Delight
6—7 servings

2½ cups bread cubes (equal parts white and rye bread)
2½ cups apple cubes
7 tablespoons butter (for frying)
salt
5 eggs
4 cups milk
4—5 tablespoons sugar
1 teaspoon ground cinnamon
butter (to grease the pan)

Fry the ¼-inch apple cubes and bread cubes in separate frying pans and let them cool. Sprinkle with a pinch of salt. Cook the milk and let cool. Beat the egg, sugar and cinnamon into the cold milk. Mix in the cubes and pour the mixture into a greased pan. Bake in the oven at 440°F. Shortly before the cake is done sprinkle its entire surface with sugar. Return to the oven and bake till done. Serve with whipped or light cream.

ÖLAND

Nettle Soup

6—7 servings

2 quarts nettles
2 quarts stock
2 tablespoons butter
3 tablespoons flour
salt
white pepper
¼ teaspoon anise
¼ teaspoon fennel
(¼ teaspoon chervil)
1 tablespoon chives
2 teaspoons butter (when soup is done)

Parboil in lightly salted water the tender leaves and leading shoots of May nettles. Grind or mince them very fine. Make a white sauce from the butter, flour and pork or calf stock, add the anise, fennel and chervil (if desired). Cook for 45 minutes, strain. Add the ground nettles, and the minced chives and season to taste with salt and white pepper. Add 2 teaspoons butter if desired. Serve the soup with poached eggs or wedges of hard-boiled eggs.

Mutton Soup

4—5 servings

1½ lbs breast of mutton or lamb
1 carrot
1 leek (only the white part)
¼ celery stalk
1 parsnip
1 tablespoon chopped parsley
2½ cups milk
1 teaspoon salt
white pepper
¼ laurel leaf
a pinch of thyme

Rinse the meat very quickly in cold water. Place in a saucepan and add cold water. Let it come to a boil and cook for 2—3 minutes. Again rinse it under running cold water until the water is completely clear. Place the meat in 1½ quarts of water and add the sliced vegetables, salt, laurel leaf and thyme. Cook the soup covered until the meat is done. Remove the meat, cut into cubes and return to the soup. Add the milk and the parsley and season to taste.

44

Potato Dumplings ("kroppkakor")

about 10 dumplings

5 lbs raw peeled potatoes
4/5 lb salted side pork cut into cubes
about 1/3 lb barley and wheat flour
  mixed
salt

Grate the raw potatoes and put in a heavy towel to let the water escape (this usually takes about 2 hours). Then mix the potatoes with the flour and some salt. Shape the dough with your hands into small rolls and fill with the pork cubes. Cook the dumplings in lightly salted water over low heat for about 45 minutes. Serve with melted butter and lingonberry sauce.

Potato Dumplings from Öland
("kroppkakor")

about 15 dumplings

4 lbs raw potatoes, peeled
1 lb cold boiled potatoes
1 lb salt pork
salt
1 large onion
2 teaspoons coarsely ground allspice
about 2/5 lb barley and wheat flour
  mixed

Cut the pork into small cubes and mix with the minced onion and the ground allspice. Grate the raw potatoes, and squeeze out the water in a heavy towel. Rice the boiled potatoes and mix with the grated ones. Add the flour and knead into a heavy dough. Shape into small rolls and fill them with the pork mixture. Flatten them slightly and boil them over low heat in lightly salted water for about 40 minutes. Serve the dumplings with melted butter and lingonberry sauce (mixed with cream if desired).

Pork Dumplings ("kroppkakor")

4 servings

2 eggs + 2 egg yolks
2½ cups flour
2 tablespoons melted margarine (for the
  batter)
2½ cups half-and-half
1 teaspoon powdered yeast
2 teaspoons sugar
½ teaspoon salt
4/5 lb lightly salted pork
2 tablespoons margarine (for frying)

Make 1 quart fairly thick pancake batter. Cut the pork into small cubes and fry. Strain off the pork fat and mix with the margarine. Heat a dumpling pan and grease it with the fat. Put the pork cubes in the batter and stir. Bake the dumplings in the pan the way you bake the small Swedish pancakes. Dilute the batter with some water if the dumplings seem to be too hard. Serve them immediately with lingonberry sauce or raw, strained lingonberries.

Roasted Spareribs

4 servings

2 lbs spareribs
2 tablespoons butter or margarine
salt
white pepper
2½ cups bouillon
1 laurel leaf
2 carrots
1 onion
4 parsley stalks
4 crushed juniper berries
1 egg
bread crumbs

Crack the bones in three or four places, salt and pepper and brown quickly. Add the bouillon and the seasonings and steam the meat under cover. Remove the meat when it is almost done, brush with the beaten egg and sprinkle with the bread crumbs. Bake in the oven until done and nicely browned. Serve with applesauce and mashed potatoes.

Skin and clean the hare, then rinse several times. Cut the body into about 8 equal parts. Salt and pepper the pieces and brown them in a Dutch oven or kettle. Add the minced onion and stir for about a minute, then sprinkle with the flour and let it get slightly browned. Add enough bouillon to cover the hare, then the laurel leaf and the juniper berries, and cook covered for about 1 hour or until the pieces are tender. Add the cream and bring to a boil again. Color the gravy lightly. Remove the meat pieces to another saucepan. Season the gravy to taste, strain, and pour over the meat pieces. Serve the stew with rowan-berry jelly and boiled potatoes.

Hare Stew

4—5 servings

1 large hare
2 tablespoons flour
1 laurel leaf
3 crushed juniper berries
1 quart bouillon
1 red onion
2 tablespoons butter
salt
white pepper
2½ cups cream

Mushroom Balls

4—5 servings

1¼ lbs parboiled chanterelles or mixed
   mushrooms
2 eggs
1/5 lb onions, sliced and sautéed
¾ cup bread crumbs
3 tablespoons flour
1 teaspoon salt
1 teaspoon white pepper
4 tablespoons butter or margarine
1 lb smoked or salted pork

Grind the mushrooms and the onions, beat the eggs slightly and add to the mushroom mixture with the bread crumbs, some flour if desired, and salt and pepper. Taste, then test the consistency by frying a sample of the mixture. Shape into small flat balls and fry. Serve with smoked pork or ordinary fried salted pork.

ERYNGIUM MARITIMUM

Anchovy Eye, Fried in Butter

4 servings

4 egg yolks
8 anchovy fillets, minced
1 tablespoon minced onion or chives
1 tablespoon minced red beets
1 tablespoon parsley
1 teaspoon capers
1 tablespoon boiled potatoes, cut into tiny cubes
1 tablespoon butter or margarine (for frying)

Mix all ingredients and shape into a hamburger-type ball. Fry quickly on both sides and serve as an hors d'oeuvre with butter, cheese and toast or as a smörgåsbord dish.

Oldfashioned Desert

4—5 servings

2 cups grated dark bread
1 tablespoon candied orange peels, chopped
4 tablespoons sugar
⅓ lb grated apples
1 cup whipping cream
3—4 tablespoons orange juice

Whip the cream. Mix all the other ingredients except the juice. Add the juice a little at a time until you reach the right consistency, moist but not runny. Put the mixture in a bowl and spread the whipped cream on top.

47

GOTLAND

Asparagus Soup from Gotland

6—7 servings

2 lbs asparagus
1 large onion
2 tablespoons butter (for frying)
2 tablespoons flour
2 quarts veal stock or water
(1 bouillon cube)
salt
1 cup light cream
1 tablespoon butter

Skin and rinse the fresh asparagus and cut into inch-long pieces. Boil the tips separately in lightly salted water. They will be used to garnish the soup. Heat the butter in a saucepan and sauté the sliced onion and the asparagus pieces. Sprinkle with the flour and stir for a couple of minutes. Add the broth from the tips and water or veal stock and cook over low heat for 1½ hours. Strain the soup and season to taste with salt and a bouillon cube if desired, add

the cream and 1 tablespoon cold butter. Add the tips just before serving the soup.

Lamb Soup with Barley Grains

5—6 servings

8 cups lamb stock
2 carrots
½ celery stalk
½ turnip
1 onion
1 leek
⅓ cup barley grains, crushed
2 tablespoons chopped parsley

Clean and rinse the roots and cut into small cubes. Rinse the grains in cold water. Bring the stock to a boil and skim. (Or use the same amount of water.) Add the roots and the grains and cook covered over low heat. Season to taste with salt and white pepper, add the parsley right before serving.

Fish Stew from Gotland

4—5 servings

2 lbs fish (small codfish, flounder etc.)
2 leeks (only the white part)
5—6 large potatoes, peeled
1 tablespoon minced chives
1 tablespoon minced parsley
1 tablespoon margarine
salt
white pepper

Clean and rinse the fish and fillet. Clean the leeks and slice, slice the potatoes. Grease the bottom of a saucepan and alternate layers of potatoes, leeks, chives and parsley. Add salt and pepper and enough water to cover. Cook covered over low heat. When the potatoes are almost done add the fish and cover with a greased paper. Continue to cook under cover till done. Season to taste with more salt and serve directly from the pot.

Simple Salmon

4—5 servings

about 2 lbs left-over salmon
2½ cups milk
¾ cup flour
1 egg
1½ cups bread crumbs
⅓ cup parsley
salt
white pepper
2 tablespoons butter or margarine

Cut left-overs of fresh or salted salmon into inch-long pieces. Soak in milk for about 30 minutes. Remove from the milk and roll the pieces first in the flour, then in the beaten egg, and finally in a mixture of the chopped parsley, salt and pepper. Fry them in plenty of fat and serve with currant sauce and boiled potatoes.

Fish Pudding

4—5 servings

2/5 lb left-over cooked fish
¾ cup rice
1½ cups water
2 eggs
2 tablespoons butter
2 cups milk
salt
white pepper
bread crumbs

Cook the rice in small amount of water and add the milk to make a porridge. Cool. Remove all skin and bones from the fish left-overs and add to the rice. Add the eggs and season to taste with salt and pepper. Grease and flour a suitable mould or pan, put the mixture in the pan, sprinkle with bread crumbs and pour melted butter over. Bake in hot oven (480°F) and serve with melted butter, a white sauce, chive sauce or mushroom sauce.

Lamb Chops with Parsley Potatoes
4 servings

1—2 lamb chops per serving
butter
boiled potatoes
red onion
bread crumbs
parsley
salt
pepper

Clean the chops thoroughly, season and fry in plenty of butter. Remove the chops and fry the sliced potatoes and the minced onion in the fat from the chops until golden brown. Sprinkle with the bread crumbs, lots of parsley and some salt. Fry the potatoes for a few more minutes, then heap on top of the chops. Serve with browned butter.

Mutton Fiddle
"Mutton Fiddle" is the name for a salted, dried and sometimes even smoked leg of mutton or lamb. (The name refers to the shape of the leg.) Mutton Fiddle is served cold, thinly sliced, as a smörgåsbord dish or as a main dish with e.g. scrambled eggs or creamed potatoes.

Jumping Embers
(This is a humorous name for grilled slices of salted, dried leg of mutton. It refers to the fact that the salt makes the slices hiss and crackle when they are put on the hot stove.)

Grill very thin slices of mutton fiddle directly on the top of the stove. The slices can be moistened with oil before grilling. Serve with scrambled eggs, creamed potatoes, or creamed potatoes with chives.

Marinated Wild Rabbit

4 servings

1 rabbit
2 tablespoons margarine
1½ cups cream
2 teaspoons potato starch

Marinade:

3 cups beer
½ cup wine vinegar
1 onion
1 carrot, sliced
1 laurel leaf
6 juniper berries, crushed
5 white peppercorns, crushed
3 allspice berries, crushed
1 teaspoon thyme

Rinse the skinned and cleaned rabbit thoroughly. Prepare the marinade, put the rabbit in the marinade and leave in a cool place for 2—4 days. Turn the meat every day. Brown the rabbit well, preferably in an oblong cast-iron kettle with a cover. Baste with the marinade during the frying. Remove the rabbit and reduce the gravy somewhat by boiling. Add the cream. Dissolve the potato starch in a small amount of water and add to the gravy while stirring. Season to taste with salt and strain. Cut the meat into serving pieces and serve with boiled or fried potatoes and rowan-berry or cranberry jel

Fancy Rabbit Stew

4 servings

1 rabbit
salt
white pepper
1 laurel leaf
2 tablespoons butter or margarine
1 red onion
1 carrot
5 allspice berries
1 teaspoon thyme
2 teaspoons molasses
2 tablespoons flour
2 cups water
½ cup cream

Rinse a skinned and cleaned rabbit thoroughly and cut into serving pieces. Salt and pepper the pieces and fry in a cast-iron kettle if available. Chop the carrot and the onion and add to the kettle, sprinkle with the flour and stir. Add the water and the other ingredients except the cream. Cook covered until the meat is done. Remove the meat and reduce the gravy a little by boiling. Add the cream, let the gravy come to a boil, strain and season to taste. Serve the rabbit with riced or mashed potatoes.

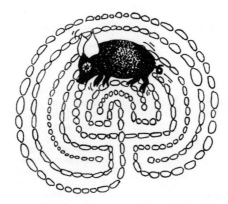

Roasted Spareribs with Ginger

4—5 servings

2 lbs fresh spareribs
2 onions
1 carrot
½ laurel leaf
parsley stalks
salt
1 tablespoon ground ginger
2 tablespoons sugar
2 eggs
bread crumbs, finely crushed
butter or margarine
2½ cups bouillon or water

Dressing:

2 eggs
1½ cups bread crumbs mixed with
2 tablespoons flour

Frying:

4 tablespoons margarine
2 tablespoons oil

Brown the meat in a kettle on top of the stove or in the oven. Add the vegetables and the laurel leaf. After about 30 minutes add the bouillon or water. Remove the meat when done, and thicken the gravy. Season to taste and add some soy sauce if needed, then strain. When the meat has cooled brush it with the beaten eggs. Mix the sugar, the ginger, and the bread crumbs. Sprinkle over the meat and roast with butter or margarine in the oven till light brown. Serve with the gravy and mashed potatoes.

Saffron Pancake

5—6 servings

1 cup milk-boiled porridge rice
6 eggs
1 cup cream
1 gram saffron
1 tablespoon flour
25 grated sweat almonds
2 bitter almonds
3 tablespoons sugar or honey
3 tablespoons butter
1/2 teaspoon cinnamon
1 pinch of salt
Cherry preserves or fresh wild strawberries with whipped cream

Beat the eggs and add the flour, cream and milk-boiled rice. Crush the saffron grate the almonds. Add almonds, saffron, honey, cinnamon and salt to the butter and mix well. Heat a frying pan, sizzle the butter and pour in the butter. Bake for about 20—25 minutes in 350—400⁰F oven. Remove the pan from the oven and let the pancake cool a little in the pan. Place on a serving platter and serve warm with cherry preserves, or fresh wild strawberries. Perhaps also with whipped cream.

Manna Groats Pudding with Orange Sauce

6—7 servings

3½ cups milk
½ cup manna groats
2 egg yolks
2 egg whites
4 teaspoons sugar
grated peel from 2 oranges

Cook the groats in the milk. Add the egg yolks and simmer the pudding till thickened. Stir in the grated orange peels and the sugar. Let cool, beat the egg whites till stiff and add to the pudding. Season to taste with more sugar. Pour into a bowl and serve with orange sauce.

Orange Sauce:
1½ cups water
½ cup sweet orange juice
1 tablespoon potato starch

Bring the water to boiling and thicken with the potato starch (diluted in some cold water). Bring to a boil again. Let cool, then add the orange juice.

Rhubarb Pancake

4 servings

1 lb rhubarb
2 eggs
4 teaspoons sugar
½ teaspoon salt
4 tablespoons butter or margarine
1½ cups flour
3 cups milk

Clean and scrape the rhubarb, cut into pieces and rinse in water. Melt the butter in a frying pan, sauté the rhubarb for a few minutes, then pour it over into a greased baking pan or ovenproof dish. Beat together the batter and pour over the rhubarb. Bake in medium hot oven. Shortly before the pancake is done, sprinkle with a thin layer of sugar, then leave the cake in the oven for a few more minutes.

ÖSTERGÖTLAND

Green Pea Soup

4—5 servings

2/5 lb lightly salted pork cut into cubes
½ cup celery root cut into cubes
2½ cups water or light bouillon
1 cup fresh or frozen green peas (or canned ones)
1 tablespoon butter
2 tablespoons flour
3½ cups milk
2 tablespoons chopped parsley
1 tablespoon cold butter
salt
white pepper

Sizzle the pork and the celery root in butter in a saucepan. Sprinkle with the flour and stir, add the water or bouillon. Add the peas and cook slowly under cover until everything is done. Add the milk and the parsley and bring to a boil once more. Season to taste with salt and pepper and stir in one tablespoon cold butter.

Cabbage Soup from Valdemarsvik

6 servings

3/5 lb fresh pork
½ turnip
2 carrots
½ celery stalk
½ a small cabbage head
1 onion
2 tablespoons chopped parsley
½ laurel leaf
4 allspice berries
2 quarts water
salt

Clean and rinse the vegetables and cut into strips. Let the pork and the water come to a boil and skim thoroughly several times. Cook for 30 minutes then add the vegetables, seasonings and a teaspoon salt. Remove the rind when the pork is done and cut the meat into small cubes. Return these to the soup and season to taste with salt. Finally sprinkle with the chopped parsley.

54

Ovenbaked Lake Trout from Lake Vättern

4—5 servings

2 lbs trout
1 lemon
dill sprigs
bread crumbs
butter
2 eggs

Stuffing:
2 large tomatoes
2 large onions
½ can mushrooms
3 tablespoons butter
salt
white pepper
1 tablespoon dill
1 tablespoon parsley

Scrape the fish and remove gills and fins. Slit open in the back and remove the backbone, clean and rinse in lightly salted water. Rub with salt and pepper. Mince the onion, peel the tomatoes and cut into large pieces. Sauté the onion, mushroom and tomatoes in butter. Add the chopped parsley and the dill. Fill the fish with this mixture and sow it together, then dip it in the beaten eggs and the bread crumbs. Bake in the oven with lots of butter for about 20 minutes. Garnish with lemon slices and dill sprigs, serve with boiled potatoes and a gravy made of the pan drippings, mushroom juice and cream.

Angel Food

4 servings

1½—2 cups heavy cream
½ cup applesauce
7—8 fancy rusks or cookies
milk
2 tablespoons raspberry preserves or jam

Whip the cream, reserve about 1/3 for garnish and mix the rest with the apple sauce. Soak the rusks in the milk and spread on the bottom of a bowl. Cover with cream, then with the sauce and decorate the top with a design of whipped cream and raspberry jam.

Married

4 servings

1 cup heavy cream
1 teaspoon sugar
2½ tablespoons lingonberry sauce (or some other suitable jam)
8 small cones (ready-made)

Whip the cream and mix with the jam. Add some sugar if desired. Fill the cones and serve immediately. The cream mixture can also be served in a bowl with small almond cookies as decoration. Fresh lingonberries, sweetened with sugar, can be substituted for the jam.

Count Spens' Cake

8 servings

1½ lbs almond paste
cream
½ cup slivered almonds
butter icing
preserved fruit (pears, peaches)
(blue and green grapes)

Soften the almond paste with some cream until it reaches a consistency where it can be spread with a knife onto a large piece of wax paper. Place the paper on a baking sheet and bake the paste at 480°F till light yellow. Divide into four identical squares and cover three of them with a thick layer of butter icing. Stack the squares on top of each other and cover the top one with a thin layer of butter icing and sprinkle with toasted almond slivers. Decorate the top with "roses" of butter icing, fruit preserves in various colors and jams. Cover the sides with toasted almond slivers.

Butter Icing:
3/5 lb butter
⅓ lb confectioners' sugar
1 egg
1/4 cup kirschwasser (German/Swiss cherry liqueur)

Cream the butter and the sugar. Add the egg and continue beating. When the icing is smooth beat in the cherry liqueur.

VÄSTERGÖTLAND

Cheese Soup

8 servings

2 tablespoons butter
2 tablespoons flour
2 quarts veal stock
a pinch of paprika
2½ cups dry grated cheese
¼ cup madeira
2 egg yolks
1 cup cream
4 hard-boiled eggs
salt
red pepper

Melt the butter and add the flour and the stock, cook over low heat for 20 minutes. Strain the soup and season with a pinch of paprika. Stir in the cheese and add the madeira, season to taste with more salt, if needed. Beat together the cream and the egg yolks and add to the soup just before serving. Serve very hot with halved hard-boiled eggs and strips of red pepper.

Fried Salmon Trout with Cream

4 servings

4 salmon trout (each of serving size)
4 tablespoons butter
flour (for dressing)
1 tablespoon dill
1 tablespoon chives
1½ cups heavy cream
salt
white pepper

Clean and rinse the fish, season and flour it and fry in the butter. Mince the dill and the chives. Remove the fish when done and place on a serving platter. Sauté the dill and the chives quickly in the pan drippings. Add the cream and cook slowly for a few minutes. Season to taste with salt and white pepper. Pour the gravy over the fish and serve with new potatoes cooked with dill or the almond-shaped potatoes from northern Sweden.

Crisp Fried Herring with Onion Sauce

4 servings

4 soaked herring fillets
1 egg
1 egg yolk
bread crumbs
flour
butter or margarine

Sauce:
1 medium red onion
1½ cups half-and-half
1 tablespoon butter or margarine
2 teaspoons flour

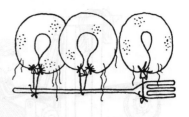

Sausage from Västergötland

about 15 servings

3 lbs fresh pork
3/5 lb lard
4/5 lb barley grains, crushed
½ tablespoon allspice, crushed
½ teaspoon ground white pepper
a pinch of ginger
2 tablespoons salt
1 teaspoon sugar
1 large onion
about 3½ cups water
sausage skin

Soak the grains in the water for about an hour. Mince the onion and grind the pork and the lard. Mix together thoroughly, season to taste. Fill the sausage skins, but not too full. Rub the sausage with a mixture of sugar and salt and keep in a cool place till the following day, when it is rinsed off in cold water. Preserve the sausage in coarse salt in a large crock. Serve boiled with mashed potatoes, baked beans or creamed green peas.

Dry the fillets and roll them in flour, beaten egg and bread crumbs. Press a little to make the dressing stick. Fry the fillets thoroughly until dark brown and crisp. Sauté the minced onion until soft, sprinkle with the flour and add the half-and-half. Season the sauce carefully (keeping in mind the saltiness of the herring). Serve with potatoes boiled in the jacket and pickled red beets.

Hare in Royal Gravy

8 servings

1 hare, skinned and cleaned
3 tablespoons margarine
3 tablespoons flour
1 carrot
1 red onion
1 laurel leaf
salt
5 allspice berries
5 white peppercorns
3 anchovies
1 teaspoon thyme
1 tablespoon molasses
2 teaspoons vinegar
1 cup cream

Rinse the hare several times, wipe completely dry and cut into serving pieces. Salt the pieces and brown them in a saucepan. Sprinkle with the flour and stir, then add enough water to cover the meat. Cook for a few minutes, then add all ingredients except the cream. Remove the meat pieces as they get done. Season the gravy to taste, and reduce it somewhat by boiling. Add the cream and cook for a few more minutes, then strain it onto the meat. Serve with lingonberries or pickled cucumber and mashed potatoes.

Egg Crullers

25—30 crullers

3 eggs
2.4 ounces sugar
1¼ cups heavy cream
2/5 lb flour
grated rind from ½ lemon

Garnish:
sugar

Beat the eggs and the sugar for 10—12 minutes, then add the cream, flour and grated lemon rind. Heat 1 lb oil, cooking fat or coconut oil. Press 1 tablespoon of the batter through a pastry bag letting it coil back and forth in the fat to make a round perforated cake about 3 inches thick. Turn it over with a perforated ladle when golden brown on the bottom side. Remove when golden brown on both sides and place on a piece of paper. Immediately sprinkle with sugar.

Fig Pudding

10 servings

2/5 lb of figs
4 egg yolks
⅓ lb sugar
1/5 lb butter
2/5 lb sweet almonds
4 bitter almonds
1 cup heavy cream
2 tablespoons flour
1/5 lb bread crumbs

Soak the figs in tepid water for a few hours, then cut them into small cubes. Scald and grind the almonds. Beat together the eggs, butter and sugar. Add the cream, then the figs, flour, bread crumbs and almonds. Pour the batter into a greased and floured pan and bake at 400°—450°F for about 45 minutes. Let cool a little before serving. Serve with whipped cream, vanilla sauce, lemon sauce, etc.

Värmland

Bean Soup from Värmland

4—5 servings

1½ cups hulled broad beans
1 onion
1 leek (only the white part)
2 tablespoons chopped parsley
3 large potatoes
2 tablespoons butter
2 tablespoons flour
salt
white pepper
1 bouillon cube
1 tablespoon butter

Hull and rinse the beans and cook in lightly salted water until soft. Chop the onion, leek and potatoes into small cubes and sauté them in the butter. Stir in the flour and then the broth from the beans. Cook the soup for about 30 minutes, add the beans and cook some more. Season to taste with salt and pepper and a small bouillon cube. Finally add the parsley and one tablespoon cold butter.

Hare Soup

5—6 servings

1 hare skinned and cleaned
1 tablespoon margarine
1 tablespoon oil
1 tablespoon flour
1 carrot
2 onions
1 leek
¹/₂ laurel leaf
1 teaspoon tomato purée
a pinch of thyme
4 white peppercorns
1¹/₂ quarts water or bouillon
(madeira or sherry)
¹/₂ cup cream
2 egg yolks
salt

Sauce:
1 quart chanterelles
3 tablespoons butter
2 tablespoons flour
2 cups half-and-half
salt
white pepper

Clean and fillet the fish, coat it with salt, pepper, beaten egg and bread crumbs. Bake in the oven and baste often with the butter or margarine. Clean and rinse the mushrooms, mince. Sauté in the butter and sprinkle with the flour. Pour the half-and-half into the pan used for baking the fish, bring

Cut off the saddle and the hind legs of the hare and keep in a cold place for later use. Cut the fore-part into 3—4 pieces. Sauté the meat and the chopped vegetables in the margarine and the oil, sprinkle with the flour, add the seasonings and the water or the bouillon. Skim a couple of times and cook over low heat for 2 hours. Remove the meat, sever it from the bones and cut into small cubes. Strain the soup and season to taste with some madeira or sherry if desired. Return the meat cubes to the soup. Beat the egg yolks into the cream and add just before serving the soup.

Oven-roasted Pike-Perch from Vänern with Chanterelle Sauce

5 servings

2½ lbs pike-perch
2 eggs
4 tablespoons bread crumbs
4 tablespoons flour
5 tablespoons butter or margarine
1 tablespoon parsley
1 tablespoon chives
salt
white pepper

to a boil, then strain it onto the mushrooms. Cook over low heat for about 10 minutes, season with salt and pepper. Sprinkle the fish with a mixture of minced parsley and chives. Serve the sauce in a gravy boat. Serve with boiled new potatoes with dill.

Creamed Perch from Vänern

6 servings

6 perches of serving size
3 tablespoons butter or margarine
1½ tablespoons flour
1 lemon
2 tablespoons dill
2 tablespoons parsley
salt
white pepper
¾ cup water

Clean, scale and rinse the fish, remove the gills but leave the head and the red fins. Grease the bottom of a suitable saucepan, sprinkle with the chopped dill and parsley. Place the fish on top, back sides up, and sprinkle with the flour and dots of butter, salt, pepper and the juice of ½ lemon. Add the water and cook covered over low heat. Season to taste when the fish is done. Serve the fish covered with the sauce in a deep dish and garnish with dill sprigs and lemon slices.

Värmland Sausage

12—15 servings

1 lb beef
1 lb pork
2/5 lb lard
3 lbs potatoes (peeled)
1½ tablespoons salt
2 teaspoons sugar
2 teaspoons white pepper
1 teaspoon allspice
1 medium onion
8 feet sausage skin

Saltpeter mixture:
1 cup salt
1 teaspoon saltpeter

Brine:
½ cup salt
2 teaspoons sugar
1 teaspoon saltpeter

Cut half of the lard into small cubes. Grind the rest and the potatoes, using next to the finest wheel in the meat grinder. Add the seasonings and mix together the ground meats. Test the consistency and the taste by frying a small sample of the mixture. Stuff the sausage skin fairly loosely. Rub the sausage with the saltpeter mixture and let rest for 12—15 hours, after which time the sausage is kept in the brine.

Cook the brine and let cool before adding the sausage. Don't crowd the sausage to keep it from discoloring.

Cinnamon Fritters
about 20

1/5 lb butter
flour
about ½ cup water
1/5 lb sugar
2 teaspoons ground cinnamon
3 eggs
½ cup water
2 cups fat (coconut oil)

Melt the butter and knead in flour until the dough is firm. Add the water and knead again. Stir in the eggs one at the time and knead the dough until it becomes elastic. Drop pieces of the dough with a dessert spoon into the hot fat (350°F). Let the fritters cook until golden brown. Roll them in a mixture of sugar and cinnamon. Serve immediately with raspberry or strawberry jam.

Frozen Cloudberry Cream
8 servings

¾ cup confectioners' sugar
½ cup water
1 quart fresh cloudberries or cloudberry jam
4 egg yolks
2 cups whipping cream

Cook the sugar and the water together in a saucepan till syrupy. Remove the saucepan from the stove and beat in the egg yolks, one at a time. Bring slowly to a boil again, stirring constantly until it becomes thick and shiny. Remove the saucepan from the stove and continue stirring until cool. Press the cloudberries through a strainer with some sugar and stir 1 cup of the purée into the sugar and egg mixture. Whip the cream until stiff and stir carefully into the mixture. Season to taste with sugar and pour into a suitable mold for freezing.

Sand Pastry
20—25 pastries

1/5 lb melted butter or margarine
1/5—¼ lb sugar
¼—⅓ lb flour
2 egg yolks
⅓ cup sweet almonds, chopped

Mix ingredients thoroughly. Grease pastry shells well and fill with the batter. Bake at 350°F for 10—12 minutes.

King Oscar's Cake
8 servings

1/5 lb sweet almonds, ground
4 egg whites
¼ lb sugar
2.4 ounces slivered almonds, toasted

Filling:
1/5 lb sugar
½ cup milk
4 egg yolks
⅓ lb butter

Grind the almonds and beat the egg whites until stiff. Carefully stir the almonds and the sugar into the egg whites. Shape the mixture into two round layers, cover with greased paper and bake in low heat. Mix milk, sugar and egg yolks in a saucepan and heat slowly till it starts to thicken, stirring constantly. Let cool slightly, then beat in the butter. Spread most of the filling on one of the cake layers, place the other one on top and cover with the rest of the filling. Sprinkle with toasted, slivered almonds.

Närke

Vegetable Soup with Rice and Pork

6 servings

3/5 lb salted side of pork
1 carrot
1 leek (white part only)
½ celery stalk
1 parsnip
2 tablespoons parsley
2 tablespoons rice
salt
white pepper
thyme
1½ quarts bouillon or water

Cut the pork into small cubes. Clean and rinse the vegetables and cut into small cubes. Fry the pork in a saucepan for a few minutes, add the vegetables and stir. Add the bouillon or the water, bring the soup to a boil and skim thoroughly. Cook the rice in water, and stir into the soup when soup is done. Season to taste with a pinch of thyme and some salt and pepper. Finally stir in the chopped parsley.

Mock Loin of Pork with Cream Sauce

6 servings

1 lb ground pork
2 eggs
milk
4 tablespoons bread crumbs
1 teaspoon anchovy sauce
1½ tablespoons cooking oil
salt
white pepper
¾ cup water

Sauce:
2½ cups milk or half-and-half
1½ tablespoons butter or margarine
1½ tablespoons flour
2 teaspoons anchovy sauce
1 teaspoon sugar

Mix together the ingredients for the meat loaf (don't let it get too loose) and season to taste. Grease a frying pan or a baking pan with the oil, shape the meat loaf and bake at 440°—480°F. When almost done carefully pour 3/4 cup water over the meat. Make the sauce, season and add the pan drippings from the meat. Cut the meat loaf and serve with the sauce, lingonberries, cucumber or red beets, and potatoes.

Innkeeper's Omelet

3—4 servings

⅓ lb smoked ham
5 eggs
2 large potatoes, boiled
1 large onion
4 tablespoons cream
salt
white pepper
1 tablespoon chopped parsley
3 tablespoons margarine

Cut the ham, potatoes and onion into small cubes. Fry the ham and remove when done. Put some margarine in the pan and sauté the onion slowly. Add the potato cubes and return the ham cubes to the pan and mix well. Beat together the eggs, parsley and cream, and some white pepper and salt. Add more margarine to the pan and pour the omelet batter onto the cubes. Stir the egg mass carefully with a fork a couple of times. Serve immediately directly from the pan.

Liver Stew

4 servings

1 1/5 lbs calf or beef liver
2 medium onions
4 tablespoons mushrooms
3 tablespoons margarine
¼ cup madeira
1 teaspoon potato starch
½ cup light cream
salt
white pepper

Slice the liver, season the slices and fry quickly in a frying pan. Mince the onions, cut the mushrooms into larger pieces, and sauté the onion and the mushrooms together. Mix liver slices, onion and mushrooms in a kettle, add water and cook covered over low heat. Skim a couple of times. Remove the liver when done, and reduce the gravy somewhat by continued cooking. Add the cream and season to taste. Dissolve the potato starch in the wine and add to the gravy while simmering. Return the liver to the sauce and bring to a boil once more. Serve with mashed potatoes or creamed spaghetti.

Stuffed Onions

4 servings

3—4 large onions
3/5 lb ground veal
1 egg
⅓ cup rice
salt
white pepper
3 tablespoons butter or margarine
1 tablespoon bread crumbs
milk
1 cup water or bouillon
1 bouillon cube

Skin and parboil the onions, separate the different layers from each other before completely cool. Cook the rice in the milk to make a porridge. Mix the ground veal, eggs, rice and seasonings. Fill every onion section with a heaping teaspoon of the meat mixture, secure with more onion and place in a greased pan. Sprinkle with the bread crumbs and dots of butter and bake at 500°F. Add the water or the stock when the meat is nearly done. The taste can be improved by adding a bouillon cube. Baste a couple of times and cover with wax paper if the heat seems to be too strong towards the end. Season the pan juices to taste. Serve with mashed potatoes.

Apple Dumplings

6 servings

6 medium apples, hard
6 tablespoons marzipan
1 tablespoon sugar
25—30 raisins
2 tablespoons granulated sugar

Dough:
2/5 lb cold butter
2/5 lb flour
½ cup water

Peel and core the apples, fill with the marzipan and the raisins, and sprinkle with sugar all around. Bake them in the oven till half done and let cool. Chop the butter and mix with the flour. Add the water and roll out the dough to a rectangular shape about ¼ inch thick. Fold into four layers, turn ¼ turn and repeat the rolling and folding three times. Roll out the dough about 1/8 inch thick and cut into squares large enough to cover one apple each. Brush with beaten egg and sprinkle with the granulated sugar. Bake until nicely browned in very hot oven (480°—520°F). Serve warm or cold with whipped cream, light cream or vanilla sauce.

SÖDERMANLAND

Ice Pike with Butter and Horseradish

4 servings

1 ice pike weighing about 2 lbs
4 tablespoons melted butter
3 tablespoons horseradish, grated
salt

Clean and rinse the fish, but do not scale it. Cook in salted water and serve with the melted butter, grated horseradish and boiled potatoes.

Boiled Whitefish with Egg Sauce

4—5 servings

2 lbs whitefish
1 small onion
4—5 dill stalks

Sauce:
1 tablespoon butter or margarine
1 tablespoon flour
about 1½ cups fish stock
1 hardboiled egg
1 tablespoon minced dill
salt

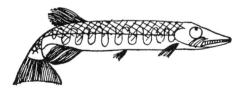

Slice the beef and the kidney evenly, salt and pepper and sauté quickly. Peel the potatoes and the onion and slice. Alternate layers of meat, kidney, potatoes and onions in a saucepan. Stir some water into the frying pan and pour into the saucepan to cover the contents. Add the bouquet garni and cook covered over low heat for about 45—60 minutes. Season to taste with salt and white pepper. Remove bouquet garni and sprinkle the stew with the chopped parsley. Serve very hot.

Creamed Summertime Spinach

4 servings

4/5 lb fresh spinach
2 tablespoons butter or margarine
2 tablespoons flour
2½ cups half-and-half
a pinch grated nutmeg
salt
(white pepper)
1 tablespoon browned butter

Clean, scale and rinse the fish and cut into serving pieces. Cook in lightly salted water together with the sliced onion and the dill stalks. Melt the butter, stir in the flour and add 1½ cups or more of the fish stock. Cook slowly for about 7 minutes. Add the chopped egg and the dill and season to taste. Serve the fish in the sauce right out of the pot with boiled potatoes.

Clean and rinse the spinach (remove all tough stalks) and chop into strips. Make a white sauce of the butter, flour and half-and-half, season it with salt and a pinch of nutmeg and cook over low heat for 10 minutes. Add the spinach and cook another 5 minutes (take care so it does not stick to the bottom of the pan) then season again. Brown the butter and add. Serve the spinach with bacon, fried pork, meat balls, cold salted ham, boiled beef, etc.

Rydberg's Stew

4—5 servings

1 1/5 lbs fillet of beef (flank, round)
3/5 lb veal kidney
1 large onion
8—10 large potatoes
1 bouquet garni (1 laurel leaf, some parsley stalks, 1 sprig of thyme, bound up in 1 green leek leaf, tied with a thin string)
salt
white pepper
2 tablespoons margarine
2 tablespoons parsley

Hashed Calf Lights

about 10 servings

1 calf heart and lung
1 onion
1 carrot
5 white peppercorns
5 allspice berries
½ laurel leaf
1 teaspoon thyme
1 teaspoon marjoram
¾ cup minced onion
6 anchovy fillets or 2—3 tablespoons anchovy sauce
3 tablespoons flour
3 tablespoons margarine
2 teaspoons vinegar
salt
water

Cut the lungs and the heart into smaller pieces and soak them in water for 2—3 hours. Cook the pieces in water together with the vegetables, salt and seasonings. Let the pieces cool in the stock, then grind them through the next to the finest gauge on the meat grinder. Sauté the onion in butter, sprinkle with the flour, add the stock and cook for a few minutes. Add the ground mixture and let the hash come to a boil slowly. Sauté the anchovy and add to the hash, season to taste with additional salt, thyme, marjoram and white pepper. Add the vinegar and taste. Go easy on the seasonings. The hash will be improved by the addition of some ground cooked veal. Serve with fried or poached eggs, red beets and boiled or baked potatoes.

Marrow Pudding with Frothy Wine Sauce

5—6 servings

1.6 ounces sweet almonds, ground
2 bitter almonds, ground
1.6 ounces seedless raisins
¾ cup bread crumbs
2½ cups milk
2.5 ounces beef marrow
3 eggs
4 tablespoons sugar
1 tablespoon brandy
a pinch of salt
4 teaspoons butter (for the pan)

Beer-Posset with Eggs
3—4 servings

2 bottles small beer — about 3 cups
4 eggs
½ cup milk
1½ tablespoons sugar
1 piece of ginger
½ teaspoon salt

Bring the small beer to a boil and
add the milk. Beat the egg yolks in a
bowl and add to beer mixture, stirring
constantly. Add the ginger, salt and
sugar. Remove from the heat and
taste. If needed the ginger can be left
in to give additional taste.

Clean, rinse and mince the marrow.
Mix the almonds, raisins and bread
crumbs into the milk. Beat the eggs
and the sugar. Mix all ingredients and
add the brandy. Grease and flour a
pan, pour in the batter and bake in a
water-bath for about 45 minutes at
440°—480°F. Serve with Frothy Wine
Sauce.

Sauce:
8 egg yolks
2½ tablespoons sugar
1¼ cups white wine
¼ cup water
the juice of 1 lemon
1 teaspoon grated lemon peel

Put all ingredients into a heavy saucepan (not an aluminum one) and beat
the sauce vigorously over medium heat
until it starts to simmer and gets thick
and frothy. Season to taste and serve
immediately.

The Queen's Compote (Jam)
8 servings

1 quart raspberries
1 quart blueberries
1¼ cups sugar
¾ cup water

Clean and rinse the berries. Make syrup
by cooking the water and the sugar,
add the berries and cook for 3—4
minutes. Remove the berries with a
perforated spatula and put in a serving
bowl. Reduce the syrup slightly by
cooking, then pour it over the berries.
Serve the compote with cream and
cookies.

Crown Princess Lovisa's Cake

10—12 servings

4 egg yolks
1½ cups sugar
1½ cups butter
1½ cups flour
5 bitter almonds
15 sweet almonds
4 egg whites
¾ cup mixed jam (blueberries and raspberries)
1 tablespoon confectioners' sugar
1 tablespoon butter or margarine (for
the pan)

Stir together the sugar and the egg yolks vigorously. Melt the butter and add. Blanch the almonds and chop finely, add to the batter together with the flour. Beat the egg whites until stiff, then add to the batter. Bake two layers at 440°—480°F. Let cool, then place on top of each other with the jam between. Sprinkle with the sifted confectioners' sugar and serve with vanilla sauce.

UPPLAND

Stewed Perch

4 servings

2 lbs perch — 4 fishes of equal size
6 tablespoons butter
2 teaspoons flour
4 tablespoons parsley
4 tablespoons dill
1 tablespoon lemon juice
2 tablespoons water
salt

Scale the fish thoroughly, clean and rinse it (leave the head and the roe, remove the gills). Grease the bottom of a saucepan and cover with the chopped parsley and dill. Salt the fish lightly and place close to each other with the back sides up. Dot with butter and sprinkle with flour, then add another layer of parsley and dill. Add the lemon juice and the water and cook covered over low heat for 12—15 minutes. Season the sauce to taste. Cook the roe separately in salted water, then add to the pan with the fish. Serve directly from the pan with boiled potatoes.

Fish Stew from Roslagen

4 servings

1 3/5 lbs eel
3/5 lb carrots
2 tablespoons margarine
salt
4 white peppercorns
4 allspice berries
1 laurel leaf

Clean, skin and rinse the eel, then cut into inch-thick slanted slices. Cut the carrots into small cubes. Sauté the fish and the carrots in a saucepan for about 5 minutes. Add the seasonings and some water and cook covered over low heat until done. Serve with boiled potatoes.

Stewed Salt Lake Burbot (Rimbo)
4—5 servings

3 lbs burbot
1 onion
1 leek
1 carrot
½ laurel leaf
6 white peppercorns
2 allspice berries
¼ mace
1 tablespoon lemon juice
1¼ cups light cream
1 tablespoon butter
1 tablespoon flour
1 tablespoon butter (to be added just before serving)

Skin, clean and rinse the fish (save the roe and the liver) and cut into inch-wide pieces. Remove the gills. Boil the fish in water together with the minced vegetables, the laurel leaf, pepper and mace (do not add salt). Add the head for extra flavor and skim carefully. Remove the pieces after about 15 minutes, leave the vegetables to cook for another 10 minutes. Strain the stock, make a small ball of the butter and the flour and simmer in the stock till thickened. Cook 5 more minutes, then add the cream. Season with the salt, lemon juice and pepper if needed, finally beat in the cold butter. Cook the roe and the liver in salted water. Return the fish to the sauce and serve straight from the pan, garnished with the sliced roe and liver and with lemon slices dipped in chopped parsley. Serve with boiled potatoes.

Grilled Bleak with Spinach
4—5 servings

2 lbs bleak
2 tablespoons oil
1½ tablespoons salt
4 tablespoons butter
1 tablespoon minced dill

Clean and rinse the fish and cut off their fins. Wipe them dry and place in a bowl. Sprinkle with the salt and add the oil. Grill the fish in a very hot and dry frying pan or directly on the clean stove. Serve immediately garnished with four slices of dill butter.

Creamed Spinach:

1 lb fresh spinach (or frozen spinach)
2 tablespoons butter or margarine
1 tablespoon flour
2 cups light cream
salt
white pepper or nutmeg

Clean and rinse the spinach (remove all thick stalks), parboil, then chop but not too finely. Sauté in the butter and sprinkle with the flour. Stir carefully, then add the cream, a little at a time. Season the spinach with salt and white pepper, or with salt and a pinch of grated nutmeg.

Cut out the core of the cabbage head, parboil the cabbage in boiled salted water. Separate the leaves and trim or cut out the thick center vein from the leaves. Rinse the rice and cook in the milk till it reaches the consistency of heavy porridge. Mince and sauté the onion. Mix the meats with the eggs, onion, milk, seasonings and rice. Season to taste. Put one to two tablespoons of the meat mixture on each leaf and roll and fold into small rolls. Place them in a greased baking pan or kettle and sprinkle with the sugar or pour the molasses over, add the melted butter. Fry the rolls on both sides over medium heat. After about 30—40 minutes add the brown gravy and cook under cover for another 30 minutes. Season the gravy to taste and serve the rolls in the gravy with mashed or boiled potatoes.

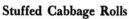

Stuffed Cabbage Rolls

4—5 servings

1 medium head of cabbage
⅓ lb ground beef
⅓ lb ground pork
about ¾ cup milk (for the meat)
2 eggs
1 onion
¼ cup rice
¾ cup milk (for the rice)
salt
white pepper
2 tablespoons sugar or molasses
3 tablespoons butter or margarine
2½ cups thin brown gravy

Brown Gravy:

2 tablespoons butter
2 tablespoons flour
2½ cups water
2 small bouillon cubes
soy sauce
(salt)
(white pepper)

Melt the butter, add the flour and frizzle till browned, then add the water, a little at a time. Cook for 7—8 minutes then add the bouillon cubes. Color the gravy with the soy sauce and season to taste with salt and white pepper if desired.

Uppsala Beef Stew

5 servings

4/5 lb boiled salted beef
1 large carrot
½ turnip
1 leek
1 onion
½ celery stalk
4 potatoes
1 laurel leaf
3 allspice berries
3 white peppercorns
salt
parsley
water or bouillon

Cut the beef and the vegetables into inch-sized cubes and cook covered together with the seasonings (do not add the potatoes until the carrots are tender). Season to taste with salt and serve sprinkled with chopped parsley.

Dannemora Porridge

5—6 servings

1 quart milk
1 egg
1 tablespoon butter
3 tablespoons sugar
1 tablespoon vanilla sugar
2 tablespoons flour
2 tablespoons potato starch

Garnish:
1 cup heavy cream
strawberry jam

Beat together the ingredients in a heavy saucepan. Place the pan on the stove and beat until the porridge is smooth. Bring to a boil slowly and cook for a few minutes beating continually. Remove the pan from the stove and continue stirring for another 5 minutes. Put in a serving bowl and let cool. Garnish with the whipped cream and the strawberry jam and serve with milk.

77

VÄSTMANLAND

Burbot Soup

4 servings

2 lbs burbot
1 quart milk
2 tablespoons butter
8 allspice berries
1 teaspoon salt
1 tablespoon chives

Skin and clean the fish and cut into inch-wide pieces. Rinse the pieces, the liver and the roe thoroughly and put them in a saucepan. Add the milk, butter, salt and the crushed allspice berries. Cook covered over low heat until done. Season to taste and add the chives. For an extra fine soup remove the fish pieces and put into a serving bowl, then strain the soup onto the fish pieces and add the chives.

Pike with Horseradish Sauce

(Creamed Pike)
4 servings

1½ lbs pike
1 lemon
3 tablespoons butter or margarine
1½ tablespoons flour
1¼ cups milk
nutmeg
1 tablespoon horseradish
salt
2 teaspoons butter

Clean and fillet the fish and cut into inch-thick slices. Cook the slices in boiling salted water with a couple of lemon slices. Melt the butter in a saucepan, stir in the flour and add ¼ cup fish stock and the milk. Sim-

mer for 10 minutes, then season to taste with salt, some nutmeg and freshly grated horseradish. Finally stir in 2 teaspoons cold butter. Place the fish pieces in the sauce and bring to a boil. Season with more horseradish if desired. Serve with boiled or riced potatoes.

Fried Perch with Currant Sauce

4 servings

4 medium perch
3 tablespoons butter or margarine
1 egg
bread crumbs
salt
white pepper

Sauce:
2 tablespoons butter or margarine
2 tablespoons flour
2 cups water
3 tablespoons currants
½ tablespoon vinegar
a pinch of white pepper
½ teaspoon salt
1½ tablespoons sugar or molasses
(soy sauce)

Scale, clean and rinse the fish. Season and dip into egg and bread crumbs, then fry in plenty of fat.
Melt the butter in a saucepan, stir in the flour and add the water. Clean and rinse the currants and add to the sauce, cook for 5 minutes. Season with the vinegar, white pepper, salt and sugar or molasses. Color with some soy sauce if desired. Serve the fish with the sauce and boiled potatoes.

Herring "En Chemise"

1 serving

1 salted Iceland or Fladen herring
1 tablespoon fried onion slices
2—3 tablespoons fat or oil
1 teaspoon butter or margarine

Clean and fillet the herring and remove the skin. Soak in water for 10—12 hours, then remove them and wipe them dry. Place the fillets on greased wax paper, spread the onion between them and fold the paper into a package in the shape of a half circle. Be sure to fold the edges well together. Place the package in a frying pan with a couple of tablespoons of warm fat and bake in a hot oven (440°—480°F) for 5—6 minutes. Baste and turn the package a couple of times. Serve the herring in the package (en chemise) to be opened at the table. Serve with potatoes cooked in their jackets.

Everyday Stew

5 servings

4/5 lb fresh brisket of beef
3 onions
2 carrots
4 potatoes
2 cabbage wedges
½ turnip
5 allspice berries
5 white peppercorns
1 laurel leaf
salt
2 quarts water or bouillon
¾ cup chopped parsley

Cut left-overs of fresh beef brisket and the cabbage, carrots, onions and potatoes into inch-size cubes. Cook everything except the potatoes covered over low heat in the water or the bouillon together with the seasonings. Add the potatoes when the roots are almost done, and cook until the potatoes are done. Finally add the parsley and season to taste.

Veal and Hazel Hen Balls

5 servings

1 large hazel hen (plucked and cleaned)
3/5 lb ground veal
1/5 lb ground lard
2 eggs + 2 egg yolks
bread crumbs
cream
½ teaspoon dried juniper berries, crushed
salt
butter or margarine

Remove all the meat from the bird and discard skin and sinews. Grind the meat twice through the finest gauge in the meat grinder. Mix the ground veal, ground hazel hen meat, ground lard, eggs, bread crumbs, and cream to desired consistency and season with salt and juniper berries (or white pepper). With a spoon dipped in warm water shape the meat mixture into oblong balls. Melt some butter in a saucepan or frying pan, put the balls in the butter and bake them in a hot oven, basting very often. Serve them in a white sauce made with cream, with mashed potatoes and currant jelly, hip jelly, cucumber pickles, lingonberries or a green sallad.

Moose Meat Balls

4 servings

4/5 lb ground moose meat
2 large red onions
2 tablespoons margarine
1 cup fine bread crumbs
1—1½ cups cream or milk
2 eggs
salt
white pepper
3 tablespoons margarine
1 tablespoon oil

The Old Charcoal-Burner's Wood Grouse

1 wood grouse (unplucked)
2/5 lb butter or margarine
8 juniper berries (dried and crushed)
1 teaspoon salt

Remove head, neck, legs and tail feathers from the grouse. Clean out the stomach cavity and wipe the bird's insides clean with a wet cloth. Fill the bird with a mixture of butter, juniper berries and salt, then sow it together with a thin piece of string. (In the old days the charcoal burners used to sow the birds together with thread made of spruce roots.) Cover the bird, feathers and all, with a thick layer of clay and bake it over a fire of charcoal and wood set in a whole in the ground. The bird will be done in about 45 minutes and the whole clay package can be removed from the fire. Carefully knock off the clay, whereupon the feathers will come off too. Open up the "seam"

Sauce:
1 tablespoon flour
(1 tablespoon margarine)
2 cups bouillon or 1 bouillon cube

Mince the onions and sauté in margarine until soft. Mix the meat with the onion and the eggs and with the bread crumbs soaked in the cream. Salt and pepper. Fry a sample meat ball to determine the right taste and consistency. Shape the balls and fry them in a mixture of oil and margarine. Beat the flour into the pan juices (add 1 tablespoon margarine if needed), then the bouillon or water and the bouillon cube. Cook the gravy for 10 minutes, then strain it onto the meat balls. Bring to a boil and season to taste. Serve with boiled potatoes, creamed or fresh vegetables, or macaroni and lingonberry sauce.

and pour out and strain the butter and the meat juices. Cut up the bird by first separating the two breast pieces, which can be sliced into smaller pieces, then the thighs, which are sliced into pieces after removing the bones. Serve the grouse with the butter and boiled potatoes.

Fried Wild Duck
4 servings

1 duck (plucked)
1 thin slice lard
2 tablespoons butter or margarine
salt
white pepper

Gravy:
3 tablespoons butter or margarine
2 tablespoons flour
1½ cups cream
1 tablespoon red currant jelly
salt
white pepper

Clean, singe and rinse the bird and bind it up. Cover the breast part with the lard, tie with a few pieces of string and salt and pepper the bird. Brown it thoroughly all around, then let it continue frying in a covered kettle over medium heat for 40—50 minutes. After 20 minutes baste with the pan juices and dilute these with 3/4 cup water.

Melt the butter in a saucepan, stir in the flour and add the pan juices and the cream. Cook the gravy for about 10 minutes, and season to taste with the red currant jelly, salt and pepper. Serve the bird carefully sliced with rowan-berry or cranberry jelly, the gravy and nicely browned potatoes.

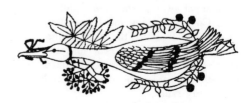

Egg Cheese Cake with Raisins
4 servings

5 eggs
2 cups milk
¾ cup raisins
½ teaspoon salt
sugar to taste
1 teaspoon lemon juice

Mix thoroughly the eggs, milk, sugar, salt and lemon juice. Strain the mixture through a steel strainer and heat slowly. Remove from the heat when it starts to curdle and beat slowly for a few minutes. Rinse the raisins and dry them, then place them in a cake pan. Pour the mixture over the raisins and place the pan in a cool place. Serve the cake after it has thickened, with vanilla or fruit syrup sauce.

Fritters
about 25

¾ cup flour
¾ cup water
2.4 ounces butter or margarine
4 eggs
2 tablespoons grated lemon peel
1 quart oil or coconut fat
½ cup sugar

Bring the water and the butter to a boil, beat in the flour and cook the mixture slowly for about 10 minutes. Let cool a little, then stir in the eggs, one at a time, and the grated lemon rind. With a spoon form small balls and cook these in the hot oil (350°F) till light brown. Place the fritters on a paper to drain. Sprinkle with sugar and serve immediately.

Dalarna

Green Beans Stew with Carrots and Pork Sausage

4 servings

3/5 lb green beans
⅓ lb small carrots
1 lb pork sausage
2 teaspoons ketchup
white pepper
salt
2 tablespoons chopped parsley

Clean and cut the carrots and the beans. Cook covered in lightly salted water for about 10 minutes. Add the pork sausage and continue cooking over low heat for 20 minutes. (Prick the sausages in a few places to prevent them from bursting.) Remove the sausage when done and slice, season the vegetables with salt, pepper, ketchup and parsley. Return the sliced sausage to the pot and sprinkle with additional parsley. Serve with boiled potatoes.

Apple-Pork

4 servings

4/5 lb fresh pork
4 large hard apples
1 tablespoon butter or margarine
6 white peppercorns
salt
3 tablespoons chopped parsley
water
(1 bouillon cube)

Cut the pork into thin slices and brown in a frying pan. Peel and core the apples and place alternate layers of pork and apples in a pan or a saucepan. Add the seasonings and enough water to cover. Simmer until all ingredients are soft. Season to taste, add a bouillon cube for stronger flavor. Sprinkle with chopped parsley and serve with potatoes cooked in their jackets.

84

Charcoal Buns (Idre)

One version of an oldfashioned dish favored by lumber-jacks, charcoal burners, and timber floaters:

flour
water
salted pork

Beat together equal parts of flour and water to a consistency of pancake batter. Cut the pork into cubes and brown in a frying pan. Pour a suitable amount of the batter over the pork cubes and stir a little so that the grease and the pork get evenly distributed. Place in the oven to bake until done. Serve with lingonberry sauce (or fresh lingonberries stirred with sugar) and cold butter. In the old days these buns were baked right on top of the glowing embers of the open fireplace in the log cabin. To get a nicely browned surface, they used to place the pan at an angle against the pile of embers, after the bun had solidified.

Roast White Grouse

4 servings

2 grouse (plucked and cleaned)
2 slices lard
3 crushed juniper berries
salt
white pepper
butter or margarine
¾ cup water or bouillon

after a complete roasting time of 40—45 minutes. Sauté the livers and the hearts in the butter in a saucepan. Sprinkle with the flour, add the bird stock and cook for 20 minutes. Strain and add the cream and the jelly. Color the gravy with some soy sauce if necessary and season to taste with salt and white pepper. Slice the birds, pour some browned butter over them and serve with the gravy, rowan-berry jelly and browned potatoes.

Gravy:
1½ tablespoons butter or margarine
1½ tablespoons flour
½ cup bird stock
1 cup cream
liver and heart from the birds
2 teaspoons red currant jelly
salt
white pepper
(soy sauce)

Rinse the birds in cold water and bind them with thin cotton string. Salt and pepper the birds and bind the slices of lard to their breasts. Brown the birds on all sides in a large kettle. (Use wooden spoons for turning them.) Let them roast slowly, turn them occasionally and baste thoroughly. After about 15 minutes add the water or the bouillon and the crushed juniper berries. After 5 more minutes remove the lard slices. The birds will be done

Potato Pancakes
4 servings

8 large potatoes
4 eggs
2 tablespoons flour
1 teaspoon salt
4/5 lb lightly salted pork

Peel and grate the potatoes. Mix in the eggs, flour and salt. Fry the pork slices and use the grease for baking the pancakes. Serve them immediately, while piping hot, with the pork and/or lingonberry sauce or fresh lingonberries stirred with sugar.

Rhubarb Dumplings
6—8 dumplings

Pie Dough:
2/5 lb margarine
1/5 lb flour
1—2 tablespoons water
1 egg

Pastry Dough:
⅓ lb butter
3 tablespoons sugar
about 2/5 lb flour

Filling:
2 tablespoons sugar
1 1/5 lbs rhubarbs

Brush with:
1 egg

Garnish:
granulated sugar

Mix together a pie dough or a pastry dough and put in a cool place for 20 minutes. Roll the dough fairly thin and cut with a knife or pastry cutter 6—8 squares. Rinse, peel and cut the rhubarbs into half-inch pieces. Place 8—10 pieces in each square, sprinkle with 1 teaspoon sugar and fold up the four corners and press the edges together. The leftover dough can be cut into long strips with the pastry cutter, placed on the dumplings and folded in the shape of a bow. Brush the dumplings with a beaten egg and sprinkle with some granulated sugar. Bake at about 500°F and serve them warm with cold light cream or vanilla sauce.

Omelet Cake

8 servings

9 eggs
6 tablespoons light cream
3 tablespoons butter
3 teaspoons sugar
3 tablespoons raspberry jam
6 tablespoons whipped cream
1 tablespoon confectioners' sugar
½ teaspoon cinnamon, ground

Beat together the eggs, cream and sugar. Divide the batter into three equal parts. Bake three flat omelets in a frying pan, without turning them over. Let them cool a little. Then place them on top of each other, separated by a layer of jam and a layer of whipped cream. Sprinkle the top with a mixture of confectioners' sugar and cinnamon. Serve the cake as a dessert.

Gooseberry Cream

4 servings

1 quart gooseberries
¾ cup sugar
2 tablespoons potato starch
4 cups water

Remove stems and blossom ends from the gooseberries and rinse them in warm water. Bring the water to a boil and add the berries, cook until tender but not yet falling apart. Add the sugar, dissolve the potato starch in small amount of water and stir into the berry mixture. Stir carefully while bringing the mixture to a boil. Season to taste with additional sugar. Serve cool with milk.

Cherry Tartlets

6 servings

6 pastry canapés
3 tablespoons cherry jam
½ cup heavy cream
30 sweet almonds

Fill the canapés with the cherry jam and press the whipped cream through a pastry bag onto the edges of the canapés. Sliver the almonds and toast quickly in a pan. Sprinkle the slivers generously onto the cherry jam. Serve the tartlets as a dessert or a coffee cake.

Thin Rye Crisps

2 lbs peeled boiled potatoes
1 teaspoon salt
2¼ cups rye flour

Pass the potatoes through a grinder or a steel sieve. Mix with the salt and the flour and knead the mixture until you get a hard dough. Roll out the dough paper thin. Prick with a fork all over. Bake on top of the stove in a frying pan. Serve the breads spread with butter and rolled up, or rolled around a slice of cheese.

GÄSTRIKLAND

Breakfast Herring

2 lbs Baltic herring (about 30)
4 tablespoons butter or margarine
salt
rye flour
8—10 juniper twigs

Clean and rinse the fish. Salt them and roll them in rye flour, then place in a frying pan with plenty of cooking fat. Immediately transfer the frying pan to a warm oven. Open the oven door after about a minute and throw a burning juniper twig into the oven. The flame will go out almost as soon as the oven door is closed and will produce a light smoke. Continue to put in burning twigs until the fish is done. Turn the fish over after 5 minutes. The smoke from the juniper twigs gives a delicious aroma to the fish. Serve with the browned butter from the pan and potatoes boiled with dill.

Chimney-Sweeps
4 servings

30—35 medium-sized Baltic herrings
1 tablespoon minced dill
4 tablespoons butter

Clean and rinse the fresh fish. Leave the fins on if the fish is not too large. Salt generously and grill directly on the hot stove or in a dry frying pan, until as dark in color as the name of the dish implies. Place them crisscrossed on a serving platter, pour some warm salted water on the bottom of the platter. Decorate with four slices of dill butter or with dill sprigs. Serve with boiled or mashed potatoes.

Smoked Herring and Eggs

6 freshly smoked herrings
1 tablespoon dill
1 tablespoon chives
2 tablespoons butter or margarine
3 eggs
¾—1 cup milk or half-and-half
½ teaspoon salt
white pepper

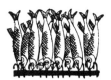

Fillet the herring and remove skin and bones. Grease an oven-proof casserole and cover the bottom with the fish fillets. Salt and pepper sparingly and sprinkle with the minced dill and chives. Beat together the eggs and the milk, season and pour over the fish. Bake for 15—20 minutes in a medium hot oven (400°F) and serve as a smörgåsbord dish.

Skin and fillet the fish. Beat together the eggs and the cream and season with the salt and the white pepper. Melt half of the butter in a heavy saucepan and pour in the egg mixture. Heat slowly and stir carefully with a wooden spoon. Remove the pan from the stove when the mixture starts to thicken. Stir in the parsley. Continue to stir a while longer, while the mixture gets somewhat thicker, and add 1—2 tablespoons cold butter if desired. Sauté the fillets quickly in browned butter. Place on a serving platter and garnish with the tomatoes cut in half and the dill sprigs. Serve with the scrambled eggs.

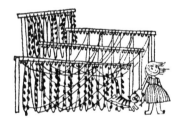

Smoked Herring Fried in Butter, with Scrambled Eggs

4 servings

8—10 freshly smoked herrings
2 tomatoes
4 dill sprigs
10 eggs
8 tablespoons cream or half-and-half
½ teaspoon salt
a pinch of white pepper
1 tablespoon chopped parsley
1/5 lb butter or margarine

Pike Loaf with Morel Sauce

6 servings

1½ lbs pike
2 teaspoons salt
¼ teaspoon white pepper
2 tablespoons flour
3½ cups heavy cream
5 egg whites

Sauce:

1—1½ quarts fresh morels
3 tablespoons butter or margarine
2 tablespoons flour
2 cups cream
½ teaspoon salt
a pinch of white pepper

Fillet the fish and pass 5 times through the finest gauge on the meat grinder. Season lightly, sprinkle with the flour and stir. Mix thoroughly and add the cream a little at a time. Beat the egg whites until stiff and stir them carefully into the fish mixture. Season with salt and pepper. Check taste and consistency by cooking a small sample. Grease an oven-proof pan and fill it with the fish mixture. Cover with greased wax paper and cook in a waterbath for 60—70 minutes at 400°F. Serve the fish loaf with the sauce and rice or boiled potatoes.

Rinse the morels and chop into fairly large pieces. Parboil them and discard the water. Sauté the mushroom pieces in the butter, sprinkle with the flour and add the cream. Cook for 8—10 minutes and season to taste with the salt and freshly ground white pepper.

Liver Pudding

6 servings

4/5 lb calf or pork liver
1/7 lb fresh pork
½ cup rice
2 tablespoons raisins
1—2 cups milk
2 tablespoons molasses
1 teaspoon salt
a pinch of white pepper
⅓ teaspoon thyme
⅓ teaspoon marjoram
2 eggs

Grind the liver and the pork. Rinse the rice thoroughly and cook in milk, parboil the raisins. Mix liver, pork, rice and raisins, and add the seasonings and the eggs. If necessary dilute with some milk, the consistency should be like that of a rather loose porridge. Test a small sample in the frying pan. Pour the mixture into a greased pan and bake at 440°—480°F until nicely browned and of firmer consistency, about 35—45 minutes. Serve very hot with melted butter and lingonberry sauce.

Fresh Lingonberry Sauce

1 1/5 lbs sugar to each 2 lbs lingonberries

Clean the berries and weigh them.
Rinse and drain well, place in a wide
crock. Add the sugar, a little at a
time, and stir until the sugar is completely dissolved and the berries crushed
and pulpy. Pour into cold preserving
jars. Cover and bind immediately.

Honey Cake
about 18 slices

⅓ lb honey
½ cup sugar
1/5 lb butter
2 eggs
1¾ cups flour
1 level teaspoon baking powder
1½ cups raisins
1 teaspoon cinnamon

Mix the honey, sugar and butter and
stir. Add the eggs, one at a time, and

stir vigorously. Mix in the raisins, sift in the baking powder, cinnamon and flour, and stir for a couple of minutes more. Grease and flour a one-quart pan and pour in the batter. Bake at about 350°—375°F. Do not cut until the following day.

Apple Cake with Nuts
16 pieces

Dough:
¾ cup milk
1 ounce yeast
1 egg
½ stick butter or margarine
½ cup sugar
3—3½ cups flour

Filling:
4 apples
¾ cup sugar
1 teaspoon cinnamon

Garnish:
2½ ounces butter or margarine
1/5 lb flour
½ cup sugar
25 chopped nuts

Dissolve the yeast in the warm milk. Stir in the egg, butter, sugar and flour and leave the dough to rise for about 20—30 minutes. Peel, core and slice the apples thinly and mix them with the sugar and the cinnamon. Mix the butter for the garnish with the sugar, flour and chopped nuts. Grease a frying-pan thoroughly and spread half of the dough on the bottom. Then a layer with the apples, then the rest of the dough and sprinkle with the garnish mixture. Let stand for 10 minutes, then bake at 400°—440°F for 40—50 minutes.

HÄLSINGLAND

Cabbage Soup

4—5 servings

½ small cabbage head
4 small carrots
1 leek
2 large potatoes
2 quarts lightly salted pork-stock
1 tablespoon parsley
1 tablespoon butter

Cut the cabbage and the leek into strips and the carrots into thin slices and cook them together with the seasonings in the stock. About 15 minutes before the soup is done cut the potatoes into strips and add. Season to taste and add 1 tablespoon cold butter and sprinkle with the chopped parsley.

Sailor's Herring

4 servings

2 salted Iceland herrings
7 large potatoes, raw
2 onions
3 tablespoons margarine

Clean and fillet the herring and remove the skin. Soak the fillets 12—15 hours. Peel and slice the potatoes and the onions. Grease a china casserole thoroughly and alternate layers of potatoes, herring, and onions, ending with a layer of potatoes. Place the casserole in a double boiler and fill it with enough water to reach the bottom of the casserole. Cook well covered.

Old Man's Delight

Old-fashioned "eats" from the heyday
of the inns and hostelries
4—5 servings

4 hard-boiled eggs, chopped
2 raw egg yolks
2 tablespoons chopped anchovy fillets
   or 2 tablespoons salted kaviar
1 tablespoon minced dill
1 tablespoon minced chives
1 tablespoon chopped parsley

Cook the bacon rinds, beef liver, onion,
barley and laurel leaf in the water
until the grains reach a thick, porridge-
like consistency. Remove the rinds, liver, laurel leaf and onion and grind
them (rather coarsely) with the left-
over meat and the anchovy. Then add
the meat mixture to the grains, season
and cook over low heat for 5 minutes.
Season carefully and if desired heighten
the flavor by adding the anchovy juice.
Serve with red beets and potatoes.

Mix the ingredients carefully in a bowl
and serve as a smörgåsbord dish. It
can also be used on grilled sandwiches.

Chopped Meat Left-overs from Norrland

6—8 servings

1 lb left-over meat, boiled (not salted)
1 lb bacon rinds
3/5 lb beef liver
1 cup barley grain
2 onions
1 teaspoon thyme
1 teaspoon marjoram
8 anchovy fillets
ground allspice
1 laurel leaf
4—5 cups water
(anchovy juice)

96

Greased Crisp-Bread

barley crisp-bread
milk
pork drippings
white pepper

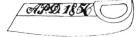

Soften the barley crisp-bread in milk
for a few minutes. Carefully remove
it to a frying pan with warm pork
drippings and heat. Season with white
pepper and add milk until it reaches
the consistency of a loose stew. Serve
instead of potatoes with fried pork.

Cloudberry Jam

fresh cloudberries
(sodium benzoate)

Clean the cloudberries and place them
in a large crock. Mash the berries with
a wooden pestle without crushing the
seeds. Pour into well cleaned wooden
kegs or jars, cover the surface with
paper dipped in paraffin wax and
cover the kegs or jars. Cloudberries
keep very well and rarely need any
preservative. If the storage area is un-
satisfactory, however, add 7 grains of
sodium benzoate for each 2 lbs of
berries.

Mashed Cloudberries

Clean the cloudberries and mash them or grind them in the meat grinder. Pass through a sieve to separate the seeds. Very ripe berries can be passed through a sieve without first being mashed or ground. Preserve the mashed berries in tightly closed bottles. Store in a dark and cool place.

Lingonberry Pears

10 lbs pears
8 lbs lingonberries
5 lbs sugar
1.8 quarts water
2 cinnamon sticks
1 vanilla stick

Clean and rinse the lingonberries. Bring the water to a boil in a large kettle, add the berries and cook covered for 10—12 minutes. Strain through a filtering-cloth. Check the volume and pour the juice back into the kettle. Add the sugar and skim thoroughly. Add the sticks of cinnamon and vanilla and cook the lingonberry juice for 10 minutes over low heat. Peel the pears and scrape the stems. (Cook small pears whole, larger ones cut in half or wedges and cored.) Put the pears in the juice and cook until tender. Remove the pears with a slotted spoon and place in jars to cool. Let the juice cool too, then pour enough of the juice over the pears to cover them completely. Bind over the jars.

Medelpad

Smoked Herring Delight

4 servings

6 freshly smoked herrings
4 large potatoes
1 large onion
butter or margarine
cream or half-and-half
salt
white pepper

Remove the skin from the smoked herrings and fillet. Cut the raw potatoes into fine strips and mince the onion. Grease an ovenproof pan and put the onion and the herring fillets on the bottom covered by the potatoe strips. Salt and pepper and add the cream. Bake in a warm oven and add some more cream during the baking if necessary.

Fried Fillet of Moose with Hunter's Sauce
4 servings

4 slices fillet of moose, each weighing
    about ¼ lb
¼ cup bouillon or water
1 quart fresh chanterelles
1 small onion
butter or margarine
1½ cups cream or half-and-half
1½ tablespoons flour
salt
white pepper

Salt and pepper the fillets and fry them in a frying pan until just done. Beat the flour into the pan drippings and add the bouillon or the water. Add the cream a little at a time and simmer the gravy for 7—8 minutes. Mince the onion and sauté in butter in a saucepan. Clean and rinse the mushrooms and cut into fairly large pieces. Sauté with the onion for about 5 minutes. Strain the gravy from the frying pan over the mushrooms and the onion, season and bring to a boil. Place the moose fillets on a warm serving platter, pour the gravy over and serve with browned potatoes.

Roasted Snow-grouse
2—3 servings

1 snow-grouse
1/5 lb butter or margarine
1 slice lard
salt
white pepper
1 cup bouillon or water

Gravy:
¾ cup bird broth
1 cup cream
1 tablespoon seasoned cheese
1 tablespoon red currant jelly
½ teaspoon salt
a pinch of white pepper
1 tablespoon flour
⅓ cup water
1 tablespoon butter

Pluck, singe and rinse the bird, wipe it completely dry. Bind up the bird and tie the slice of lard onto the breast. Use thin cotton yarn. Salt and pepper the bird and brown it quickly on all sides in an iron kettle or a Dutch oven. Lower the heat and continue browning under cover. After 15 minutes add the bouillon or the water. Baste often during the roasting. The roasting time depends on the age of the bird and could vary from 20 to 25 minutes. Remove the bird when done and cut off the breast and the thighs, returning the rest to the kettle. Add the cream, cheese and jelly. Stir the flour into the water,

Pastor's Bread

slices of coffee bread
butter
(jam)
(whipped cream)

Cut a length of coffee bread into uniform slices. Fry them quickly in butter in a frying pan until golden brown. Serve them as they are with coffee, or garnish with a good jam and serve with whipped cream.

beat the thickener into the gravy and cook for 10 minutes. Season the gravy and strain, finally add 1 tablespoon cold butter. Slice the breast pieces at an angle and not too thinly, and cut the thighs into two pieces. Place on a serving platter and garnish with whole sprigs of parsley. Serve the bird very hot (pour some melted butter over just as you are serving it) with the gravy, browned potatoes, cucumbers and jelly.

101

Härjedalen

Salmon Trout and Manna Groats Porridge

4 servings

1½—1¾ lbs salmon trout
salt
white pepper
4 tablespoons butter or margarine
2 tablespoons minced dill
1 lemon

Manna Groats Porridge:
4 cups cream or milk
¼ lb butter or margarine
⅓ cup manna groats
¾ cup flour
1 teaspoon salt
1 teaspoon sugar

Clean and scale or scrape the fish, and rinse quickly in cold water. Salt and pepper, roll it in flour and fry in plenty of cooking fat. Garnish with the minced dill and the lemon wedges.

Bring the cream and the butter to a boil. Cook the groats in the cream for a while, then beat in the flour. Cook the porridge over low heat for 8—10 minutes, stirring constantly, until it is swimming in fat. Salt and sugar and serve with the fish. Manna groats porridge can also be served with cinnamon, sugar, cold milk and thin rye crisps.

Simple Hare Loaf

6—8 servings

1 medium hare (skinned and cleaned)
1½ cups minced chanterelles
3 tablespoons minced onion
2 eggs and 2 egg yolks
about 1 cup cream or milk
¾ cup bread crumbs
1 teaspoon salt
a pinch of white pepper

Cut off all the harer's meat from the bones and remove all thicker membranes and sinews. Grind the meat three times in the meat grinder. Sauté the chanterelles and the onion in butter, cool and add to the ground meat. Add the eggs, bread crumbs and cream and mix until you have a consistency that is slightly looser than for meat balls. Season to taste and put the mixture in a greased and floured loaf pan. Cover with greased wax paper and bake in a medium hot oven for 60—70 minutes. (If a baking pan is being used it should be put in a water-bath during the baking). Prick the loaf to see if it is done. Serve with gravy made with cream or milk, and with lingonberries and, if desired, pickled cucumber.

Moose Sauerbraten

about 10 servings

4 lbs moose flank
1/5 lb lard
3 tablespoons oil or fat
salt
2 tablespoons flour
1 cup cream

Marinade:
1 quart small beer
1 tablespoon vinegar
4 white peppercorns
2 allspice berries
1 laurel leaf
5 crushed juniper berries
1 sliced onion
1 sliced carrot

Cut the meat into 2—3 pieces and the lard into thin strips, lard the pieces and bind them with thin string. Mix together the ingredients for the marinade. Put the meat in the marinade and soak for 4—5 days. Heat the cooking fat in a roasting pan, salt the meat and brown it on all sides. Sprinkle with the flour and let it brown. Add 1 cup of the marinade and the seasonings and the vegetables, add another cup or so later during the roasting. Dilute with water if the marinade seems to be getting too strong. Remove the meat when done. Add the cream to the gravy and season to taste. This should give about 1 quart of gravy.

Serve the roast with lingonberries, mashed raw and passed through a sieve, pickled cucumber, and mashed potatoes.

Stuffed Apples

6 servings

6 equally large, firm apples
⅓ cup cherry or other type jam
3 eggs
4 tablespoons sugar
1.6 ounces sweet almonds, ground

Peel the apples and core them. Fill with the jam and place in a greased pan. Beat the egg yolks and the sugar, beat the egg whites till stiff and add to the yolks and the sugar. Stir in the almonds and pour the mixture over the apples. Bake the apples for about 20 minutes at 440°F. Serve warm.

Baked Apples with Cinnamon Milk
4 servings

4 large, hard apples
2 tablespoons raisins
2 tablespoons sugar
2 tablespoons butter
2 tablespoons molasses
bread crumbs

Cinnamon Milk:
1 quart milk
1 teaspoon ground cinnamon
1 tablespoon butter

Core the apples. (Do not peel.) Brush the apples with the melted butter and roll them in the bread crumbs. Place the apples in an ovenproof pan and fill with the raisins and the sugar. Place a dot of butter on top of each apple and pour the molasses in coils around them. Bake slowly in the oven and serve warm or cold with warm cinnamon milk.

Remove when cool and fill with the jam. Press the whipped cream through a pastry bag around the edges of the shells.

Cloudberry Shells
about 20

2 cups cloudberry jam
1 cup whipped cream

Dough:

½ lb flour
⅓ lb butter or margarine
1/7 lb (2.3 ounces) sugar
1 egg

Make the half puff paste the usual way and let rest in a cool place for 20 minutes. Roll out the dough and line muffin tins or shell molds with it. Bake in a medium hot oven (440°F) and let the shells cool in the molds.

Simple Rosettes
about 25

1 egg
1½ tablespoons sugar
¾ cup half-and-half
¾ cup flour
½ cup sugar (for garnish)

Beat the egg, add the sugar and continue beating for another minute. Mix in the half-and-half and the flour. Heat the fat and dip the rosette iron into it. Then dip it in the batter and back to the fat. Hold the iron in the fat until the rosette is golden brown. Remove the iron and put the rosette on absorbent paper to drain. Roll in sugar after a short while. Serve as a coffee cake, with some tasty jam if desired.

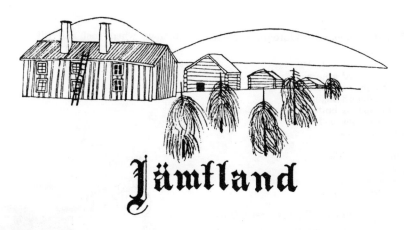

Jämtland

Simple Game Bird Soup

4 servings

a couple of game bird carcasses (grouse,
    ptarmigan, wood-grouse, etc.)
2 minced carrots
2 minced onions
3 tablespoons margarine
1 minced leek (only the white part)
1 teaspoon tomato puré
½ laurel leaf
5 white peppercorns
a pinch of thyme
2 tablespoons flour
1½ quarts light bouillon or water
½ cup cream
salt
soy sauce
(brandy, madeira or sherry)

Brown the chopped-up carcasses, add
the vegetables and the seasonings and
let them brown with. Sprinkle with the
flour and stir. Add the water or the
bouillon (made from a bouillon cube)
and bring to a boil. Skim thoroughly
and cook the soup over low heat for
2 hours. Strain and add the cream.
Color the soup dark brown with some
soy sauce and season carefully. For
stronger flavor add some brandy, madeira or sherry.

Fried Saibling with Mushroom Rice
4—5 servings

1 3/5 lbs saibling
½ cup rice
¾ cup parboiled or preserved chanterelles
1 hardboiled egg, chopped
1 tablespoon chopped parsley
4 tablespoons butter or margarine
flour
salt
white pepper

Clean, scrape and rinse the fish. Salt, turn over in flour and fry in plenty of cooking fat. Cook the rice in water. Drain off the water and mix the rice with the parsley and the chopped egg. Mince the chanterelles and sauté in butter. Salt and pepper the chanterelles, then mix them with the rice and season to taste. Sprinkle the fish with some parsley and serve with the browned cooking fat and the mushroom rice.

Heat the salmon in a saucepan with a small amount of water. Cover with greased wax paper and a potcover. Melt the butter and mix in the minced dill. Garnish the salmon with dill and parsley sprigs and lemon wedges and serve with the melted butter and boiled potatoes from northern Sweden. (The melted butter can be substituted by browned butter.)

Hot-Smoked Salmon with Potatoes
5—6 servings

2 lbs hot-smoked salmon
2/5 lb butter
2 tablespoons minced dill
dill sprigs
parsley sprigs
1 lemon

Wash and trim the tongues thoroughly. Place in cold, salted water and bring to a boil. Skim thoroughly and add the seasonings and the roots. Cook slowly covered until tender. Skin and trim the tongues. Cream the canned peas in butter, flour and half-and-half and dilute with some of the pea juice if necessary. Serve the tongue sliced the long way with the creamed peas and riced potatoes.

(Boiled tongues are also often served with a wine sauce and creamed spinach.)

Boiled Reindeer Tongue with Creamed Peas

4—5 servings

2—3 reindeer tongues
2 onions
2 carrots
1 laurel leaf
5 white peppercorns
5 allspice berries
2 teaspoons salt
1 tablespoon chopped parsley
1 can green peas
3 tablespoons butter
3 tablespoons flour
1½ cups half-and-half
(pea juice)

Castle Stew

5 servings

10 moose steaks each about 2.5 ounces
10 peeled potatoes, raw
5 medium onions
2 bottles beer or small beer
1 laurel leaf
5 white peppercorns
2 allspice berries
⅓ teaspoon thyme
salt
white pepper
3 tablespoons oil or cooking fat (for browning)
2 tablespoons parsley

Pepper and salt the steaks and brown them well. Slice the potatoes and slice and sauté the onions. Alternate layers of meat, onion and potatoes in a saucepan, pour the beer over and bring to a boil. Skim thoroughly and add the seasonings and more water or beer if needed. Cook covered until the meat is tender. Serve the stew piping hot sprinkled with chopped parsley.

Boiled Salted Pork with Fresh Cabbage

4—5 servings

2 lbs salted, lean pork
1 quart water
3 small cabbage heads
2 medium onions
8 white peppercorns
8 cloves
1 laurel leaf
8—10 peeled potatoes, raw
1 teaspoon salt

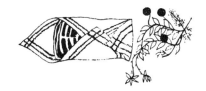

Remove the rind from the pork and cut the pork into inch-size cubes. Bring them to a boil and skim thoroughly, then continue to cook covered for 15 minutes. Split the cabbage along the core and cut about 6 wedges out of each head. Stud the onions with the cloves and place the cabbage, onions and seasonings on top of the pork. Add some more water if needed. After 5 more minutes of cooking add the cubed potatoes and cook the stew until done. Season to taste with more salt if needed. Remove the onions and serve the dish directly from the pan.

ÅNGERMANLAND

Baltic Herring Fried with Cream

4 servings

2 lbs fresh Baltic herring
1½ cups cream
4 peeled tomatoes
butter or margarine
bread crumbs
flour
2 eggs
salt

Clean and rinse the fish, leaving the backbone. Score each fish lightly on the sides, and salt them. Roll them first in the beaten eggs, then in a mixture of bread crumbs and flour, and fry them until golden brown. Add the cream and the cubed tomatoes. Simmer over low heat for a few minutes, then serve with boiled potatoes.

Hunter's Stew

4 servings

8 moose steaks each about 2.5 ounces
8 large peeled potatoes, raw
2 large onions
½ laurel leaf
a pinch of thyme
4 white peppercorns
4 allspice berries
salt
water
soy sauce

Slice the potatoes and peel and slice the onions. Flatten out the steaks somewhat and alternate layers of steaks, onions and potatoes in a large kettle. Add the seasonings and the water. Bring to a boil, skim thoroughly and continue cooking covered until done. Season to taste and color with soy sauce.

Potato Dumplings ("kams") from Angermanland

5 servings

4 lbs peeled potatoes, raw
¾ cup flour
¾ cup barley flour
1 lb salted pork

Grate the potatoes and let drain in a strainer or a towel. Mix the potatoes with the flour to make a firm dough. Cut the pork into small cubes. Shape the dough into small rolls and fill each one with 1—2 tablespoons of the pork cubes. Cook the dumplings for 45 minutes in salted water and serve them immediately with melted butter and lingonberry sauce. To make sure that the dumplings have the proper taste and consistency (the concentration of starch in the potatoes can vary considerably) it is advisable to first cook and taste a sample.

Apples au Gratin

4 servings

6 apples
½ cup chopped sweet almonds
½ cup sugar
2/3 stick butter or margarine
1 tablespoon flour

Syrup:
1½ cups water
1 cup sugar

Peel and core the apples and cut into wedges. Cook slowly in the syrup, remove when done and let drain. Grease an oven-proof platter and place the apple wedges on it. Mix all the other ingredients in a saucepan and bring to a boil while stirring constantly. Spread this mixture over the apples and bake until light brown at 440°F. Serve warm, with cold cream if desired.

Apple Meringue

4 servings

6 apples
1 tablespoon butter or margarine
⅓ cup sugar

Meringue:
3 egg whites
6 tablespoons sugar
25 scalded sweet almonds, cut into
   strips

Peel and core the apples and cut into wedges. Melt the butter and the sugar together. Place the apple wedges in the butter and sugar mixture and cook slowly until tender. Place on an oven-proof platter. Beat the egg whites until stiff and carefully mix in the sugar. Pour the meringue mixture over the apples, sprinkle with the almond strips and bake until light yellow at 340°— 390°F. Serve warm with cold cream.

Manna Groats Pudding

(Beatin' Pudding)

6 servings

¾ cup manna groats
1½ cups sweet lemonade
3 cups water
(sugar)

Bring the water to a boil. Beat the manna groats into the water and cook slowly while stirring for 5 minutes. Add the lemonade, a little at a time, continually beating. Season to taste with sugar if desired. Pour the pudding into a serving bowl, continually beating until it is light and fluffy. Serve with cold milk.

Parsonage Pastries

30 pastries

⅓ lb flour
9/10 stick butter
3 tablespoons light cream
1 egg
granulated sugar

Cream the butter and mix in the cream and the flour. Let the dough rest in a cool place for 20 minutes. Roll out the dough, cut into narrow strips and shape into the figure 8 or a rounded B. Beat the egg with some water and brush the pastries. Roll them in the granulated sugar and bake for 8—10 minutes at 480°F.

Västerbotten

Salmon Soup

5 servings

head, backbone and fins from 1 medium
  salmon
1½ quarts water
5 parsley sprigs
3 dill sprigs
2 teaspoons salt
5 white peppercorns
2—3 tablespoons barley grain
2 carrots
¼ turnip (about 2/5 lb)
1 leek
2 tablespoons minced parsley
1 tablespoon minced dill

Rinse the grains and soak them in water for 8—10 hours. Rinse the salmon head (remove the gills), the backbone and the fins and cook with the parsley and dill sprigs and the white pepper in lightly salted water for 45—60 minutes. Strain the stock and bring again to a boil. Skim thoroughly and add the barley. Cook for about ½ hour, then add the vegetables cut into small cubes. Cook until barley and vegetables are tender. If there is any meat left on the salmon head and backbone,

remove and chop and return to the soup. Season to taste and sprinkle with the minced parsley and dill. Serve with bread and butter and aged Västerbotten cheese.

Boiled Salmon Trout
5—6 servings

2 lbs salmon trout

Stock:
1 sliced onion
a couple of dill stalks
1 tablespoon vinegar
5 white peppercorns
½ laurel leaf
1 quart water
2 teaspoons salt

Sauce:
2½ tablespoons butter
2 tablespoons flour
1¾ cups fish stock
½ cup cream
2 egg yolks
2 tablespoons minced dill
salt
white pepper

Clean and wipe out the salmon trout and cut into serving pieces. Mix the stock and cook for 20 minutes. Add the fish pieces to the stock and simmer until the fish is done. Melt the butter, stir in the flour and add the fish stock, cook for 10 minutes. Add the cream, and when the sauce is again brought to a boil beat in the egg yolks. Remove the pan from the fire and season with salt and pepper, add the minced dill. Place the fish on a serving platter and garnish with dill and lemon slices. Serve with the sauce and boiled potatoes.

Mountain Whitefish Marinated in Dill
4—5 servings

2 lbs whitefish
½ cup salt (not iodized)
⅓ cup sugar
1 tablespoon crushed allspice
¾ cup chopped dill

Clean and fillet the fish. Remove all bones, but leave the skin. Rinse the fillets quickly in cold water. Mix together the salt, sugar and allspice and sprinkle the mixture along the meaty sides. Spread the dill on top of the salt mixture and place the fish with the meaty sides together. Put in a pan, cover with a plate and leave to "mature" in a cool place for 8—12 hours. Turn the fillets once during this time and add some dill if necessary. Serve the marinated whitefish cut into ¼-inch slices, garnished with dill sprigs and with the sauce, described here below.

Sauce:
5 egg yolks
4 tablespoons prepared mustard
3 tablespoons sugar
4 tablespoons minced dill
½ tablespoon vinegar
1 teaspoon salt
½ teaspoon white pepper
(cold water if desired)

Beat the egg yolks until smooth and add the sugar, salt, white pepper and vinegar. Finally stir in the minced dill.

Grilled Salted Salmon Trout with Currant Sauce

4 servings

1—1 1/5 lbs salmon trout
1 egg
flour
bread crumbs
butter or margarine

Sauce:
2 tablespoons currants
2 cups water
1 tablespoon butter
1 tablespoon flour
2 teaspoons molasses or sugar
2 teaspoons vinegar

Cut the side of the trout into serving pieces and soak in water for 15—20 minutes. Remove the pieces and wipe them dry, then turn them over in flour, beaten egg and bread crumbs. Fry slowly in plenty of cooking fat.

Clean and rinse the currants in cold water and cook until tender in 2 cups of water. Melt the butter, stir in the flour and add the currant broth. Cook the sauce slowly for 10 minutes, then season to taste with vinegar and molasses. Add the currants and bring to a boil. Serve the fish with the currant sauce and boiled potatoes.

Kidney Balls with Creamed Green Beans

4—5 servings

2/5 lb veal kidney without fat
1/5 lb beef
1/5 lb pork
2 tablespoons sliced onions, browned
2 eggs + 1 egg yolk
salt
white pepper
bread crumbs
½ cup milk
(1 bouillon cube)
1 2/5 lbs fresh green beans
1 tablespoon chopped parsley

Cream Sauce:
2 tablespoons butter or margarine
3 tablespoons flour
1 cup milk
½ cup vegetable stock
½ teaspoon salt
a pinch of white pepper

TJÄRDAL

Grind the potatoes and let the water drain off. Mix the potatoes with enough flour to make a firm dough. Sauté the pork and the kidney cubes. Shape the dough into balls the size of meat balls and fill them with the cubes. Cook the dumplings in salted water for 30—40 minutes and serve with fried pork slices and hot fat or butter.

Liver Dumplings ("palt")
about 50

4 lbs potatoes
1 lb calf or pork liver
about 4 lbs barley flour
½ quart milk
1 tablespoon salt
1 lb fresh pork

Grind the kidney, beef and onions and mix with the eggs, seasonings, bread crumbs, and milk. Shape into small balls and fry. Make a gravy by stirring in some flour and water into the pan juices. Add a bouillon cube for flavor. Cut the beans straight across into fine strips and cook in water. Make a thick white sauce from the butter, flour, milk and some of the vegetable stock. Season the sauce and stir in the well drained beans. Serve the kidney balls in the gravy, with the creamed beans sprinkled with chopped parsley.

Peel the potatoes raw and grind with the liver. Mix in the milk and the salt and stir in enough flour to make a fairly firm dough. Cut the pork into cubes and salt lightly. Cover hands with flour, take a handful of the dough and flatten it out. Put some pork cubes in the middle of the piece of dough and shape into a round roll. Cook the dumplings in salted water for about 45 minutes. Serve with lingonberries and/or melted butter.

Luxury Dumplings ("palt")
4—5 servings

2 quarts peeled potatoes, raw
barley flour
1/5 lb salted pork, cut into cubes
1/5 lb pork kidney, cut into cubes
4/5 lb salted pork
salt
butter or margarine

NORRBOTTEN

Chanterelle Soup from Norrland

6 servings

3 lbs reindeer brisket (or other less
  expensive cuts of reindeer)
2 quarts water
1 carrot
1 parsnip
1 onion
1 leek
½ celery root
1 quart chanterelles
3 tablespoons butter
1 cup cream
2 tablespoons flour
salt

Chop the meat into smaller pieces and
rinse them in cold water until thoroughly clean. Place the water and
meat in a saucepan and bring to a
boil. Skim thoroughly, cut the vegetables into pieces and add with 1
teaspoon salt. Cook the meat and the
vegetables covered over low heat and
remove when done. Strain the stock
and reduce it somewhat by additional

boiling to get a stronger flavor. Figure
about 1 1/2 quarts stock for the soup.
Clean and rinse the mushrooms and
cut into smaller pieces. Sauté in butter for a few minutes, sprinkle with
the flour and stir. Add the reindeer
stock and cook the soup for 30 minutes.
Add the cream and simmer the soup
for a short moment. Remove from the
heat and season to taste with salt.
Serve the meat and the vegetables as
separate dishes.

Boiled Mountain Saibling

5—6 servings

2 lbs mountain saibling

Stock:
1 tablespoon vinegar
1 sliced onion
1 sliced carrot
5 dill stalks
5 white peppercorns
1 teaspoon salt
1 quart water

Clean the fish and rinse carefully. Mix the stock and cook for 20 minutes. Add the fish and simmer for a few minutes. Leave standing for about 8—10 minutes before serving. Serve with melted butter and boiled Norrland potatoes.

Fried Salmon Roe

4 servings

1 lb salmon roe
butter or margarine
flour
bread crumbs
1 egg
1 cup mayonnaise
1 tablespoon dill
2 even teaspoons mustard
a pinch of white pepper

Stock:
1 tablespoon vinegar
1 quart water
1 laurel leaf
1 sliced onion
1 sliced carrot
5 dill stalks
2 teaspoons salt
6 white peppercorns

Mix the stock and cook the roe in it. Remove the roe and let drain and cool. Cut into slices, season and turn the slices in flour, beaten egg and bread crumbs. Fry them in plenty of butter, place on a serving platter and garnish with lemon and parsley. Mix the mayonnaise with the minced dill, mustard and white pepper. Serve the roe slices with the mayonnaise mixture and boiled Norrland potatoes.

Stock:
2 tablespoons vinegar
1 onion
1 carrot
7—8 dill stalks
6 white peppercorns
½ laurel leaf
salt
about 1 quart water
mayonnaise
(fresh cucumber)

Clean the fish, scrape or scale it and rinse quickly in cold water. Slice the onion and the carrot thinly and cook in the water with the dill, vinegar and seasonings for 20 minutes. Skim thoroughly and add the fish, either whole or in slices about 1 inch thick. Bring slowly to a boil, skim carefully and let the fish cool in the stock. Place the fish in a bowl or a deep dish, pour plenty of stock over it and garnish with dill sprigs. Serve with mayonnaise, (fresh preserved cucumber when in season) and boiled Norrland potatoes.

Cold Preserved Mountain Fish
4—5 servings

2 lbs fish (saibling, salmon trout, whitefish)

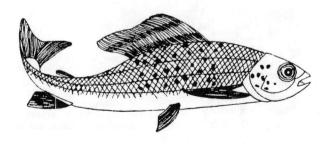

Pancake Torte

4 servings

3 cups milk
1½ cups flour
1 tablespoon butter or margarine
3 eggs
3 teaspoons sugar
½ teaspoon salt
butter or margarine (for frying)

Filling:
1 cup jam, fruit sauce or mashed, sweetened fresh berries

Garnish:
1¾ cups heavy cream
(almonds or nuts)

Beat together the ingredients for the pancake batter and let stand for 2—3 hours. Bake ordinary thin pancakes. Place them on top of each other with a layer of jam, fruit sauce, or mashed and sweetened fresh berries between every or every two pancakes. Cut the torte into serving pieces and garnish each piece with whipped cream just as they are served. If desired sprinkle the whipped cream with toasted almond slivers or toasted chopped nuts. Serve warm and with some extra whipped cream in a bowl on the side.

Pancake Pastries

about 20

2 eggs
¾ cup flour
¾ cup sugar
¾ cup melted butter or margarine
butter or margarine (for frying)

Garnish:
20 sweet almonds
1½ tablespoons granulated sugar

Cream the butter, add the eggs, one at a time, the sugar and the flour. Toast the almonds, chop them and mix with the granulated sugar. Heat and butter the Swedish pancake pan and place about 1 tablespoon of the batter in each section. Spread the batter so it fills the entire section and sprinkle with almonds and sugar. Bake in a medium hot oven (430°—440°F) until light brown. Remove the cakes with a spatula or a knife and bend them over a cane while still hot.

Sour Rusks

40—50

3 cups sour milk
2 ounces yeast
3 tablespoons sugar
1/5 lb grease or cooking fat
1 teaspoon salt
1 1/5—1 2/5 lbs coarse rye flour
flour (for rolling out the dough)
bread seasonings according to taste
(fennel-seed, anise, cardamom)

121

Heat the milk slightly. Dissolve the yeast in the sugar and mix with the milk. Add the seasonings and the fat, knead in the rye flour and let dough rise. Shape into long thin rolls (use only wheat-flour for rolling out the dough). Place the rolls on a greased cookie sheet, prick them and let rise. Bake in medium hot oven, then cut them into slices of desired thickness. Cut them in two if you want smaller rusks. Toast and dry the rusks in the oven.

Frying-Fat Buns
about 20

1 lb ordinary coffee bread dough
1/5 lb butter or margarine
3 tablespoons sugar
grated rind from 2 oranges
1 quart frying fat
sugar

Knead the butter, sugar and orange rind into the dough. Add some flour if needed. Shape the dough into small balls about the size of a silver dollar. Cook the balls in the frying fat, then roll them in sugar. Serve immediately.

Honey Cake
10 servings

2/5 lb honey
1/3 lb demerara sugar or ordinary sugar
1/4 lb (1 stick) butter
3 eggs
1 tablespoon grated orange rind
1 tablespoon grated lemon rind
1 teaspoon ginger
1/2 teaspoon cloves
1 teaspoon cinnamon
a pinch of salt
2/5—1/2 lb flour
1 teaspoon baking powder
(10—15 sweet almonds)

Heat the honey until liquid. Cream the butter and the sugar, then mix in the honey. Add the eggs, one at the time, and stir the mixture vigorously for a while. Add the remaining ingredients, leaving the flour mixed with the baking powder till last. Pour the batter into a greased long baking pan. Sprinkle with coarsely chopped sweet almonds if desired. Cover the cake with a greased wax paper and bake at 390° —440°F. Prick the cake to decide when it is done. This cake is by many considered to improve by waiting for a few days before serving.

Snow Cake

about 10 pieces

7 egg whites
½ lb sugar
¼ lb flour
1 tablespoon potato starch
1/5 lb butter
butter (to grease the pan)
10 sweet almonds, slivered (to sprinkle
   in the pan)

Beat the egg whites until stiff and mix
in the sugar. Add the flour mixed with
the potato starch. Melt the butter and
cool, then pour into the batter. Bake
the cake in a well greased pan sprinkled with almond slivers at 390°—
440°F.

Oat Cookies

about 30 cookies

¾ cup flour
¾ cup sugar
1½ cups oatmeal
¾ cup butter or margarine
¾ cup raisins
1 teaspoon bicarbonate or soda

Knead together all the ingredients.
Shape the dough into small balls and
flatten them with a fork. Bake a sample cookie to determine the consistency
of the dough and add more flour if the
cookie tends to spread out too much.
Bake in medium hot oven (390°—
440°F).

1673

Lappland

Snow-Grouse Soup

4—5 servings

1 snow grouse
3 tablespoons butter or margarine
2 tablespoons flour
2 onions
2 carrots
½ + ½ quart water
1 tablespoon red currant jelly
salt
white pepper
(¼ cup madeira)
1½ cups light cream
(soy sauce)
1 tablespoon cold butter

Roast the bird in an iron kettle until almost done. Remove it and sauté the chopped up vegetables in the kettle for a few minutes. Sprinkle with the flour and let it get browned while stirring constantly. Add ½ quart water and bring the soup to a boil. Return the bird to the kettle and cook it in the soup for ½ hour. Remove the bird, cut the meat from breast and thighs and dice. Return the carcass to the soup. Add another ½ quart water and cook the soup for 30—35 minutes. Strain the soup and season to taste with the jelly, salt and pepper and some madeira if desired. Finally add the cream. Color the soup dark brown with some soy sauce. Add the diced bird meat and stir in 1 tablespoon cold butter. Serve the soup very hot.

Midnight Sun Sandwich

4 servings

thin rye crisp bread
2 tablespoons butter
2 fillets salted Iceland herring
   (freshened)
4 tablespoons sour cream
3 tablespoons dill
2 tablespoons chives
4 hardboiled eggs

Break the bread and shape into 4″ × 4″ squares. Spread the pieces with butter and place 7—8 pieces of herring on each one (cut them like pickled herring pieces). Mix the sour cream with the dill and the chives and spread enough of it on each piece to cover the herring. Chop the whites and the yolks separately. Make a midnight sun of chopped egg yolk in the middle of each sandwich and make the sunrays by alternating chopped pieces of egg white and egg yolk.

Arctic Circle Sandwich

4 servings

4 large slices soft, white bread
2/5 lb freshly smoked reindeer roast
1½ cups canned chanterelles
butter or margarine
2 tablespoons flour
¾—1 cup cream
3 tablespoons grated cheese
salt
white pepper

Cut the reindeer roast into fine, 1-inch long strips. Sauté them for just a few seconds in hot butter and remove. Chop the chanterelles and sauté them for a few minutes in the same hot butter. Return the reindeer meat and sprinkle with the flour. Add the cream and simmer for a few minutes, season to taste with salt and pepper. Cut the crust off the bread slices and fry the slices until light brown. Cover the slices completely with the creamed reindeer meat and sprinkle with plenty of grated cheese. Place the sandwiches in a hot oven (520°F) for a few minutes and serve them immediately.

Baked Mountain Saibling

4—5 servings

2 lbs saibling
white pepper
butter, margarine or oil
browned butter
1 lemon

Clean, rinse and scrape the fish very carefully. Salt and pepper and place in a well greased and heated pan. Bake the fish in a medium hot oven, baste often during the baking, then place it on a serving platter without cutting into serving pieces. Garnish with lemon wedges and serve with browned butter and boiled (Norrland) potatoes.

125

Mustard Sauce for Marinated Salmon Trout

5 servings

2 tablespoons Swedish mustard
1 tablespoon sugar
1½ tablespoons vinegar
5 tablespoons cooking oil
(a pinch of white pepper)
3 tablespoons minced dill

Stir together the mustard, sugar and vinegar. Slowly mix in the oil while stirring constantly. Finally add the dill.

Mountain Saibling Fried in Paper

4 servings

2 lbs saibling
4 tablespoons butter or margarine
2 tablespoons minced dill
2 tablespoons minced parsley
2 minced red onions
salt
white pepper
melted butter

Clean and fillet the saibling and rinse the fillets quickly in cold water. Butter a piece of paper towel or wax paper per serving. Place one serving of fillets on each paper, salt and pepper, then cover with 1 tablespoon butter, ½ tablespoon mixed dill and parsley, and

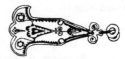

1 teaspoon minced red onions. Fold into small packages, fry the packages in a frying pan over low heat for about 5 minutes, then place the frying pan in a hot oven for a few minutes. Serve the fish in the packages (do not unfold until ready to eat) and very hot, with melted butter, minced red onion and boiled Norrland potatoes.

Reindeer Roast with Cream Gravy and Rowan-berry Jelly

7—8 servings

4 lbs reindeer roast
salt
½ cup oil
1½ quarts water or bouillon
8 juniper berries
6 tablespoons butter
6 tablespoons flour
2½ cups reindeer stock
2½ cups cream
soy sauce

Clean the meat and wipe it with a wet cloth. Bind the roast with thin string to make it keep its shape. Brown the meat in hot oil, preferably in an iron kettle with a cover. Sprinkle with

salt, after 10 minutes add the water or the bouillon and the dried and crushed juniper berries. Braise the meat in the bouillon until tender. Baste often and turn it now and then during the roasting. Reduce the stock by boiling to about ½ quart. Melt the butter in a pan, stir in the flour and add the stock and the cream, cook the gravy over low heat for 10 minutes. Season to taste with some salt and color with some soy sauce. Strain the gravy and beat for a while until smooth and shiny. Slice the roast evenly and serve with the gravy and steaming boiled potatoes, rowan-berry or cranberry jelly or pickled cucumber.

Fried Reindeer Slices

4 servings

1 lb frozen fresh reindeer sirloin or shoulder
2 medium onions
butter or margarine
salt

Carve thin slices of solidly frozen reindeer meat with a sharp knife and fry immediately with the sliced onions in a very hot frying pan and plenty of browned cooking fat. Stir with a fork, when the meat is nice and crisp place it in a serving bowl and season only with salt. Serve as hot as possible with boiled, peeled Norrland potatoes.

Oven-Baked Pancake with Cloudberry Jam

4 servings

4 eggs
2 cups light cream
3 tablespoons flour
1 tablespoon sugar
a pinch of salt
1½ cups cloudberry jam

Beat the eggs, add the cream, flour, sugar and salt and let the batter stand for 2—3 hours. Grease a frying pan with high edges or a baking pan, pour in the batter and bake for about 30 minutes at 440°—480°F. Pass the cloudberry jam through a fine steel sieve, then beat until smooth and shiny. Serve the pancake piping hot with the cloudberry jam.

Blueberry Pudding

4—5 servings

1 pint blueberries
1 cup sugar
½ teaspoon salt
2 cups water
about ½ cup flour or manna groats

Clean and rinse the berries and place in a saucepan, add the water. Bring to a boil very slowly and simmer for about 5 minutes. Add the sugar and shake the pan so that the berries will mix well with the sugar. Stir or beat in the flour, a little at a time. Do not let the berries boil while adding the flour. Then cook slowly for 10 minutes. Serve warm with milk. Many people prefer this dish cooked with manna groats rather than with flour.

Rolled Waffles

½ cup heavy cream
1 cup water
1¼ cups flour
½ cup sugar
1 tablespoon butter
1 egg yolk
½ tablespoon vanilla sugar

Melt the butter and mix all the ingredients. Heat a waffle-iron and place a normal amount of batter on it. Remove the waffles when golden brown and roll.

Cinnamon Slices

16 slices coffee bread
⅓ lb butter
4 tablespoons sugar
4 teaspoons ground cinnamon

Cut thin slices from a loaf of coffee bread (the bread can be a few days old). Spread with plenty of butter and sprinkle with a mixture of the sugar and the cinnamon. Bake the slices for a few minutes in a very hot oven and serve them immediately with coffee or tea or as a dessert.

The Provinces of SWEDEN

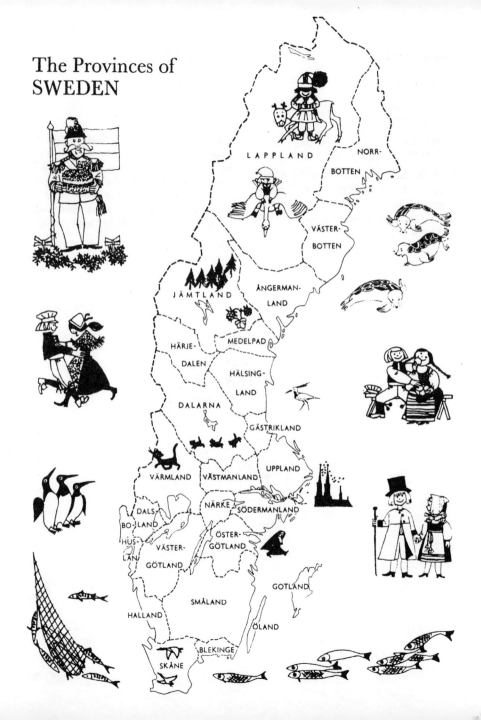

LAPPLAND

NORR-BOTTEN

VÄSTER-BOTTEN

ÅNGERMAN-LAND

JÄMTLAND

MEDELPAD

HÄRJE-DALEN

HÄLSING-LAND

DALARNA

GÄSTRIKLAND

VÄRMLAND

VÄSTMANLAND

UPPLAND

NÄRKE

SÖDERMANLAND

DALS-BO-LAND

HUS-LÄN

VÄSTER-GÖTLAND

ÖSTER-GÖTLAND

GOTLAND

SMÅLAND

HALLAND

ÖLAND

BLEKINGE

SKÅNE

Index

Anchovy Eye, Fried in Butter
(Öland) 47
Angel Food (Östergötland) 55
Apple Cake from Åmål (Dalsland) 38
Apple Cake with Nuts (Gästrikland) 94
Apple Dumplings (Närke) 68
Apple Meringue (Ångermanland) 112
Apple-Pork (Dalarna) 84
Apple Rings, Deep-Fat Fried
(Bohuslän) 35
Apples au Gratin (Ångermanland) 112
Apples, Baked, with Cinnamon Milk
(Härjedalen) 105
Apples, Stuffed (Härjedalen) 104
Arctic Circle Sandwich (Lappland) 125
Asparagus Soup from Gotland 48

Bean Soup from Värmland 61
Beans Stew, Green, with Carrots and
Pork Sausage (Dalarna) 84
Beer-Posset with Eggs
(Södermanland) 72
Beef Stew from Skåne 18
Bird Soup, Simple Game
(Jämtland) 106
Black Broth with Giblets (Skåne) 10
Bleak, Grilled, with Spinach
(Uppland) 75
Blueberry Pudding (Lappland) 128
Boar Roast, Mock Wild, with Morel
Sauce (Skåne) 14
Bread Soup (Blekinge) 22
Broth, Black, with Giblets (Skåne) 10
Buns, Frying-Fat (Norrbotten) 122
Burbot Soup (Västmanland) 78
Burbot, Stewed Salt Lake (Rimbo)
(Uppland) 75

Cabbage, Red (Skåne) 17
Cabbage Rolls, Stuffed (Uppland) 76
Cabbage Soup (Hälsingland) 95
Cabbage Soup from Skåne 9
Cabbage Soup from Valdemarsvik
(Östergötland) 54

Cake, Omelet (Dalarna) 88
Cake, Snow (Norrbotten) 123
Calf Lights, Hashed (Södermanland) 71
Castle Stew (Jämtland) 108
Chanterelle Soup from Norrland
(Norrbotten) 118
Charcoal Buns (Idre) (Dalarna) 85
Cheese Soup (Västergötland) 57
Cherry Pancakes (Blekinge) 24
Cherry Tartlets (Dalarna) 89
Chicken Soup (Dalsland) 36
Chimney-Sweeps (Gästrikland) 90
Cinnamon Fritters (Värmland) 64
Cinnamon Sauce (for Curd Cake)
(Småland) 43
Cinnamon Slices (Lappland) 129
Cloudberries, Mashed (Hälsingland) 98
Cloudberry Cream, Frozen
(Värmland) 64
Cloudberry Jam (Hälsingland) 97
Cloudberry Shells (Härjedalen) 105
Cod Roe, Fried (Halland) 26
Cod Stew from Falkenberg
(Halland) 26
Codfish, Creamed Dried (Blekinge) 23
Cod Pudding, Dried (Blekinge) 23
Count Spens' Cake (Östergötland) 56
Crab, Creamed (Bohuslän) 32
Crayfish, Sea, Soup (Bohuslän) 31
Crayfish Soup (Småland) 39
Cream Puffs (Småland) 43
Crisp-Bread, Greased (Hälsingland) 97
Crisp Fried Herring with Onion Sauce
(Västergötland) 58
Crisps, Thin Rye (Dalarna) 89
Crown Princess Lovisa's Cake
(Södermanland) 73
Crullers (Skåne) 19
Curd Cake from Småland (Bodafors) 42

Dannemora Porridge (Uppland) 77
Deep-Fat Fried Apple Rings
(Bohuslän) 35

Dessert, Oldfashioned (Öland) 47
Duck, Fried Wild (Västmanland) 82

Eel, Broiled Salted, (Blekinge) 22
Eel, Cooked Salted, with Mustard
  Sauce (Skåne) 12
Eel, Fresh, on Straw (Skåne) 13
Eel, Smoked, and Skåne Potatoes
  (Skåne) 13
Eel Soup (Blekinge) 21
Eel Soup (Skåne) 10
Eel, Steamed Smoked, with Scrambled
  Eggs and Chives (Halland) 27
Eel with Curry (Skåne) 12
Egg Cake with Smoked Pork
  (Skåne) 15
Egg Cheese Cake with Raisins
  (Västmanland) 83
Egg Crullers (Västergötland) 59
Eggs, Scrambled (Gästrikland) 91
Eggs, Scrambled, Country Style
  (Halland) 30
Embers, Jumping (Gotland) 50
Everyday Stew (Västmanland) 80

Fancy Pike Perch (Dalsland) 37
Fig Pudding (Västergötland) 60
Fillet, Fried, of Moose, with Hunter's
  Sauce (Medelpad) 100
Fish Pudding (Gotiand) 49
Fish Soup, Clear (Blekinge) 21
Fish Stew from Gotland 49
Fish Stew from Roslagen (Uppland) 74
Fritters (Västmanland) 83
Fritters, Cinnamon (Värmland) 64
Frying-Fat Buns (Norrbotten) 122

Goose, Cured, with Horseradish Cream
  or Wine Sauce (Skåne) 17
Goose, Roast, from Skanör (Skåne) 16
Gooseberry Cream (Dalarna) 88
Green Pea Soup (Östergötland) 54
Griddle Cake with Oatmeal and Apples
  (Dalsland) 38
Grouse, Roast White (Dalarna) 85
Grouse, Roasted Snow- (Medelpad) 100
Grouse, Snow-, Soup (Lappland) 124

Grouse, The Old Charcoal-Burner's
  Wood (Västmanland) 81

Hare in Royal Gravy
  (Västergötland) 59
Hare, Ragout of (Småland) 40
Hare Stew (Öland) 46
Heart's Delight (Småland) 43
Hen Balls, Veal and Hazel
  (Västmanland) 80
Herring, Baltic, Fried with Cream
  (Ångermanland) 110
Herring, Breakfast (Gästrikland) 90
Herring, Crisp Fried, with Onion Sauce
  (Västergötland) 58
Herring "En Chemise"
  (Västmanland) 79
Herring, Pottery Plate (Skåne) 9
Herring, Sailor's (Hälsingland) 95
Herring, Smoked, and Eggs
  (Gästrikland) 91
Herring, Smoked, Delight
  (Medelpad) 99
Herring, Smoked, Fried in Butter, with
  Scrambled Eggs (Gästrikland) 91
Honey Cake (Gästrikland) 93
Honey Cake (Norrbotten) 122
Horse-radish Mayonnaise
  (Halland) 27
Hunter's Stew (Småland) 40
Hunter's Stew (Ångermanland) 110
Hunting Soup (Småland) 39

Ice Pike with Butter and Horse-radish
  (Södermanland) 69
Innkeeper's Omelet (Närke) 67

Jam, Cloudberry (Hälsingland) 97
Jam, The Queen's Compote
  (Södermanland) 72
Jelly Roll (Bohuslän) 35

Kidney Balls with Creamed Green Beans
  (Västerbotten) 116
King Oscar's Cake (Värmland) 65

Lake Trout, Ovenbaked, from Lake
  Vättern (Östergötland) 55

Lamb Chops from Kalmar
  (Småland) 41
Lamb Chops with Parsley Potatoes
  (Gotland) 50
Lamb Soup with Barley Grains
  (Gotland) 48
Lamb Stew (Halland) 29
Lingonberry Pears (Hälsingland) 98
Lingonberry Sauce, Fresh
  (Gästrikland) 93
Liver Dumplings (Västerbotten) 117
Liver Pudding (Gästrikland) 92
Liver Stew (Närke) 67
Luxury Dumplings (Västerbotten) 117

Mackerel, Boiled, with Gooseberry
  Sauce (Bohuslän) 34
Mackerel, Pickled (Bohuslän) 34
Manna Groats Porridge 102
Manna Groats Pudding
  (Ångermanland) 113
Manna Groats Pudding with Orange
  Sauce (Gotland) 53
Married (Östergötland) 56
Marrow Pudding with Frothy Wine
  Sauce (Södermanland) 71
Meat Left-overs, Chopped, from
  Norrland (Hälsingland) 96
Midnight Sun Sandwich (Lappland) 125
Mock Loin of Pork with Cream Sauce
  (Närke) 66
Mock Wild Boar Roast with Morel
  Sauce (Skåne) 14
Moose Meat Balls (Västmanland) 80
Moose Sauerbraten (Härjedalen) 103
Mountain Fish, Cold Preserved
  (Norrbotten) 120
Mountain Saibling, Baked
  (Lappland) 125
Mountain Saibling, Boiled
  (Norrbotten) 119
Mountain Saibling Fried in Paper
  (Lappland) 126
Mountain Whitefish Marinated in Dill
  (Västerbotten) 115
Mushroom Balls (Öland) 46
Mushroom Rice 107
Mussel Soup (Bohuslän) 31

Mustard Sauce (Skåne) 13
Mustard Sauce for Marinated Salmon
  Trout (Lappland) 126
Mutton Fiddle (Gotland) 50
Mutton Soup (Öland) 44

Nettle Soup (Öland) 44

Oat Cookies (Norrbotten) 123
Oldfashioned Dessert (Öland) 47
Oldfashioned Fried Salmon
  (Blekinge) 23
Old Man's Delight (Hälsingland) 96
Omelet Cake (Dalarna) 88
Onions, Stuffed (Närke) 68
Oven-Baked Pancake with
  Cloudberry Jam (Lappland) 128
Oven-rosted Pike-Perch from Vänern
  with Chanterelle Sauce
  (Värmland) 62

Pancakes, Cherry (Blekinge) 24
Pancake from Småland 41
Pancake, Ovenbaked, with Cloudberry
  Jam (Lappland) 128
Pancake Pastries (Norrbotten) 121
Pancakes, Potato (Dalarna) 86
Pancake, Rhubarb (Gotland) 53
Pancake, Saffron (Gotland) 52
Pancakes, Spinach (Halland) 30
Pancake Torte (Norrbotten) 121
Pancakes, Vanilla (Dalsland) 38
Pancakes, Yeast (Skåne) 19
Parsonage Pastries
  (Ångermanland) 113
Pastor's Bread (Medelpad) 101
Pastries, Pancake (Norrbotten) 12
Pastries, Parsonage (Ångermanland) 113
Pears, Lingonberry (Hälsingland) 98
Perch, Creamed, from Vänern
  (Värmland) 63
Perch, Fancy Pike (Dalsland) 37
Perch, Fried, with Currant Sauce
  (Västmanland) 79
Perch, Stewed (Uppland) 74
Pike Loaf with Morel Sauce
  (Gästrikland) 92

Pike-Perch, Oven-roasted, from Vänern
  with Chanterelle Sauce
  (Värmland) 62
Pike with Horse-radish Sauce
  (Västmanland) 78
Plaice Fillets, Boiled, with Morel
  Sauce (Bohuslän) 33
Pork, Apple- (Dalarna) 84
Pork, Boiled Salted, with Fresh
  Cabbage (Jämtland) 108
Pork, Curried, from Skåne 15
Pork Dumplings (Öland) 45
Pork, Mock Loin of, (Närke) 66
Pork Stew from Skåne 16
Porridge, Dannemora (Uppland) 77
Porridge, Manna Groats (Härjedalen)
  102
Potato Dumplings (Småland) 42
Potato Dumplings from Ångermanland
  111
Potato Dumplings (Borgholm)
  (Öland) 45
Potato Dumplings from Öland
  (Gårdby) 45
Potato Pancakes (Dalarna) 86
Potatoes, Skåne 13
Pottery Plate Herring (Skåne) 9
Pudding, Blueberry, (Lappland) 128
Pudding, Dried Cod (Blekinge) 23
Pudding, Fig (Västergötland) 60
Pudding, Fish (Gotland) 49
Pudding, Liver (Gästrikland) 92
Pudding, Manna Groats, with Orange
  Sauce (Gotland) 53
Pudding, Manna Groats
  (Ångermanland) 113
Pudding, Marrow, with Frothy Wine
  Sauce (Södermanland) 71
Pudding, Salmon, from Halland 28

Rabbit Loaf, Simple (Härjedalen) 103
Rabbit, Marinated Wild (Gotland) 51
Rabbit Soup (Värmland) 61
Rabbit Stew, Fancy (Gotland) 51
Ragout of Hare (Småland) 40
Raisin Sausage (Skåne) 11
Reindeer Roast with Cream Gravy and
  Rowan-berry Jelly (Lappland) 127

Reindeer Slices, Fried (Lappland) 128
Reindeer Tongue, Boiled, with Creamed
  Peas (Jämtland) 108
Rhubarb Dumplings (Dalarna) 87
Rhubarb Pancake (Gotland) 53
Roast Goose from Skanör (Skåne) 16
Roast Venison (Skåne) 18
Rosettes, Simple (Härjedalen) 105
Rusks, Sour (Norrbotten) 121
Rydberg's Stew (Södermanland) 70

Saffron Pancake (Gotland) 52
Saibling, Fried, with Mushroom Rice
  (Jämtland) 107
Saibling, Mountain, Fried in Paper
  (Lappland) 126
Sailor's Steak (Halland) 28
Salmon, Boiled, with Cream Sauce
  (Halland) 27
Salmon, Fried, Oldfashioned
  (Blekinge) 23
Salmon, Hot-Smoked, with Potatoes
  (Jämtland) 107
Salmon Pudding from Halland 28
Salmon Roe, Fried (Norrbotten) 119
Salmon, Simple (Gotland) 49
Salmon Soup (Halland) 25
Salmon Soup (Västerbotten) 114
Salmon Trout and Manna Groats
  Porridge (Härjedalen) 102
Salmon Trout, Boiled
  (Västerbotten) 115
Salmon Trout, Fried, with Cream
  (Västergötland) 57
Salmon Trout, Grilled Salted, with
  Currant Sauce (Västerbotten) 116
Sand Pastry (Värmland) 65
Sandwich, Arctic Circle
  (Lappland) 125
Sauce, Chanterelle (Värmland) 62
Sauce, Cinnamon (for Curd Cake)
  (Småland) 43
Sauce, Cream (Halland) 27
Sauce, Cream (Närke) 66
Sauce, Currant (Västmanland) 79
Sauce, Currant (Västerbotten) 116
Sauce, Egg (Södermanland) 69

Sauce, Fresh Lingonberry
  (Gästrikland) 93
Sauce, Gooseberry (Bohuslän) 34
Sauce, Horse-radish (Västmanland) 78
Sauce, Hunter's (Medelpad) 100
Sauce, Morel (Skåne) 14
Sauce, Morel (Halland) 29
Sauce, Morel (Bohuslän) 33
Sauce, Morel (Gästrikland) 92
Sauce, Mustard (Skåne) 13
Sauce, Mustard, for Marinated Salmon
  Trout (Lappland) 126
Sauce, Onion (Västergötland) 58
Sauce, Orange (Gotland) 53
Sauce, Parsley (Dalsland) 37
Sauce, Wine (Skåne) 17
Sausage from Västergötland 58
Sausage, Pork (Dalarna) 84
Sausage, Raisin (Skåne) 11
Sausage, Värmland 63
Shells, Cloudberry (Härjedalen) 105
Shrimp au Gratin (Bohuslän) 32
Snow Cake (Norrbotten) 123
Sole, Ovenbaked (Bohuslän) 33
Soup, Asparagus, from Gotland 48
Soup, Bean, from Värmland 61
Soup, Bread, (Blekinge) 22
Soup, Burbot (Västmanland) 78
Soup, Cabbage (Hälsingland) 95
Soup, Cabbage, from Skåne 9
Soup, Cabbage, from Valdemarsvik
  (Östergötland) 54
Soup, Chanterelle, from Norrland
  (Norrbotten) 118
Soup, Cheese (Västergötland) 57
Soup, Chicken (Dalsland) 36
Soup, Clear Fish, (Blekinge) 21
Soup, Crayfish (Småland) 39
Soup, Eel (Blekinge) 21
Soup, Eel (Skåne) 10
Soup, Green Pea, (Östergötland) 54
Soup, Hunting (Småland) 39
Soup, Mussel (Bohuslän) 31
Soup, Mutton (Öland) 44
Soup, Nettle (Öland) 44
Soup, Rabbit (Värmland) 61
Soup, Salmon (Halland) 25
Soup, Salmon (Västerbotten) 114

Soup, Sea Crayfish (Bohuslän) 31
Soup, Snow-Grouse (Lappland) 124
Soup, Vegetable, with Rice and Pork
  (Närke) 66
Sour Rusks (Norrbotten) 121
Spareribs, Boiled Salted, with Parsley
  Sauce (Dalsland) 37
Spareribs, Roasted (Öland) 46
Spareribs, Roasted, with Ginger
  (Gotland) 52
Spitcake, Good Old (Skåne) 20
Spinach, Creamed Summertime
  (Södermanland) 70
Spinach Pancakes (Halland) 30
Stone Cakes with Fried Pork
  (Skåne) 15
Sugar Cakes (Blekinge) 24

Tartlets, Cherry (Dalarna) 89
The Queen's Compote (Jam)
  (Södermanland) 72
Thin Rye Crisps (Dalarna) 89
Torte, Pancake (Norrbotten) 121
Turbot Fillets, Broiled, with Horse-
  radish Mayonnaise (Halland) 27

Uppsala Beef Stew (Uppland) 77

Vanilla Pancakes (Dalsland) 38
Veal and Hazel Hen Balls
  (Västmanland) 80
Vegetable Soup with Rice and Pork
  (Närke) 66
Venison Meat Loaf with Morel Sauce
  (Halland) 29
Venison, Roast (Skåne) 18
Värmland Sausage 63

Waffles, Rolled (Lappland) 129
Whitefish, Boiled, with Egg Sauce
  (Södermanland) 69
Whitefish, Mountain, Marinated in Dill
  (Västerbotten) 115
Whiting Fillets, Stuffed (Bohuslän) 34
Wine Sauce, Frothy (Södermanland) 72

Yeast Pancakes (Skåne) 19

Gravad lax

(cured, marinated salmon)

Fillet about 1 1/2 kg (3 lb) salmon from the middle part of the fish. Remove all small bones but not the skin. Mix 4 tbl sugar, 4 tbl salt and 2 tsp crushed white peppercorns. Rub the salmon with most of this mixture.

Place a layer of dill at the bottom of a shallow dish and then one salmon fillet with the skin downwards. Cover with a generous layer of dill. Sprinkle with the remainder of the spice mixture. Place the other salmon fillet on top, skinside upwards, and so that the thin part rests on the thick part of the lower piece. Cover with a generous layer of dill and, finally, place a very light weight on top (the juice must not be pressed out of the salmon). Refrigerate the salmon for 1 or 2 days. Turn the salmon over when half of this time has passed.

Scrape off all the spices when the salmon is to be served. Cut it into slices. Serve with cold *gravlax* sauce, lemon wedges and boiled potatoes or with potatoes cooked in white dill sauce.

Cold mustard sauce

for the *gravad lax*

Mix 2 tbl mustard, 1 tbl sugar and 1 tbl vinegar in a bowl. Then add 6 tbl oil, a little at a time until well blended. The sauce will thicken rapidly and must be stirred vigorously. Finally add 6 tbl fermented cream and plenty of finely chopped dill.

Soft gingerbread with fermented cream

Mix 75 g butter and 2 dl brown sugar until light and fluffy. Add 2 eggs. Mix 3 dl wheat flour, 1 1/2 tsp baking powder, 1 tsp ground cinnamon, 1/2 tsp ground cloves and 1 tsp ground ginger and stir into the batter together with 1 1/2 dl fermented cream, 2 tbl orange marmelade and 10 chopped sweet almonds. Pour the batter into a buttered and breaded baking tin with a volume of approximately 1 1/2 litres. Bake the cake in an oven at 150–175°C (300–350°F) for approximately 1 hour. Invert the cake on a wire cake rack. Let stand until cold.

Filbunke

4 servings

(Bowl of fermented milk)

Heat 1/2 litre (1 pint) of milk until it is just on the point of boiling (to prevent the fermented milk from curdling). Then cool the milk to normal room temperature (22°C/72°F). Mix in 3 tbl fermented milk and 3 tbl thick cream. Pour into bowls. Cover the bowls and let them stand at room temperature until they have set, e.g. over a night. Then place the bowls in a refrigerator and let them remain there until they are to be served.

Serve with ground ginger and crushed gingerbread biscuits.

All recipes by The Farmers' Test Kitchen.

The Provinces of SWEDEN

NORR-BOTTEN

VÄSTER-BOTTEN

LAPPLAND

ÅNGERMAN-LAND

JÄMTLAND